Ignite Your Potential

22 Tools for Peak Performance and Personal Development

Inspired by travel, training and the tarot.

Copyright © 2016 Mark Carter

All rights reserved. No part of this book may be reproduced or transmitted in any form or by any means whatsoever without express written permission from the author, except in the case of brief quotations embodied in critical articles and reviews.

Published by Glow International

First Edition 2016

ISBN: 978-0-9954139-0-0

Illustrations by Deborah Gillham

Edited by Alexandra English

www.markcarter.com.au

Instagram: @ignitingyourpotential

FB: Mark Carter – Igniting Human Potential

Acknowledgements

Thank you, Deb, for the magnificent, inspiring, artistic creations. Like minds and all that jazz. A new outlet is required in lieu of our daily creative calls. ('Project 2' awaits your magic Mademoiselle!)

Big thanks to the woman with the big red pen keeping order: Alexandra English. Your surname alone destined you as an editor! Thanks for keeping my creative ramblings in check.

Thanks also to Nathan Cayless, former captain of the Parramatta Eels and New Zealand rugby team, for his insight in an earlier blog article that has been repurposed for the chapter on Authenticity.

To Jo Wilkinson-Way, 'The Boss', grazie for serendipitously steering me towards my path.

In dedication to Paolo Fortini: Florence, always stunning, may never quite feel the same without your presence Sir.

Table of Contents

Foreword..7
Potential..11
Self Confidence......................................12
Self Control..22
Attitude..30
Wellness...36
Present...44
Self Reflection.......................................50
Tonics...58
Decisions..66
Adaptability...74
Goals..82
Productivity...92
Consistency..102
Creativity...112
Collaboration.......................................118
Challenge...124
Strength...132
Acceptance...138
Gratitude...148
Authenticity..156
Candour...164
Kindness..172
Love..178
Character...188
Passion...194

Foreword

There are many aspects of life I love. Travel, development, and creativity are right up there which is why this book, my first, blends all three.

In a former life as a Contiki Tour Director, I was fortunate enough to travel extensively, often in leadership roles. I spent many years traversing Europe, an experience that became like an educational, exciting merry-go-round. My fascination with culture, traditions and history led me to stumble on the origins of the Tarot while I was living in France and Italy.

The Tarot is made up of the Minor Arcana and Major Arcana cards. These translate to 'little secrets' and 'big secrets' respectively. The Minor Arcana cards can be traced back to the Middle Ages where they were used as playing cards. They were typically comprised of four suits: cups, coins, swords and bats. In more recent times, the bat suit has been replaced with the stick suite, but apart from that, the principle of the cards is the same.

The Major Arcana cards are a little different. Their origins are shrouded in mystery, but there has been speculation that the Tarot could be traced back to the Holy Land of Israel or even Ancient Egypt. The Major Arcana cards represent the big picture life messages and themes.

Put aside the shenanigans of charlatans, over-the-top occultism and fortune telling fantasies. A simpler, more pragmatic way of utilising the idea of Tarot is as a tool for self-analysis.

In our adapted version each card has a dedicated theme and symbol to help you reflect, review, reconcile and re-engage during different stages of your life.

As I mentioned, I love development. I've worked in my field for close to 20 years and wanted to release a creative piece that simultaneously provokes personal reflection, growth and evolution. Each chapter focusses on a specific theme, which is brought to life through a story or insight. In addition to being entertaining and educational, hopefully, it will provoke awareness, thought, and action.

Ignite Your Potential is a creative development tool with a holistic spin on the concept of the Major Arcana: 22 chapters, 22 themes and 22 visual tools to encourage and inspire you to ignite your potential.

I collaborated with a wonderful illustrator, Deborah Gillham, to bring my vision to this body of work to life. You'll also notice an evolution of colour that aligns to the themes of balancing the seven chakras.

Red:

The root chakra. The Muladhara chakra. It harmonises basic survival, logic, order, vitality and passion.

Orange:

The sacral chakra. The Swadhisthana chakra. It is symbolic of compassion, desire and taste.

Yellow:

The solar plexus chakra. The Manipura chakra. It relates to creativity and personal and professional success.

Green:

The heart chakra. The Anahata chakra. It bridges low and high energy centres and is associated with self-respect, altruism, kindness and relationships.

Blue:

The throat chakra. The Vishuddhi chakra. It represents listening, thinking and communication.

Indigo:

The third eye chakra. The Ajna chakra. It focuses on the higher plane of consciousness, imagination, wisdom and authenticity.

Violet and white light:

The crown chakra. The Sahasrara chakra. It represents collective consciousness, joy, grace, optimism, fulfillment and universal love.

Potential is a priceless treasure, like gold. All of us have gold hidden within but we have to passionately dig to get it out.

- Joyce Meyer

Questions to ask yourself in order to ignite the spark and release your potential:

- What inspires me?
- What are my talents?
- What am I capable of?
- What's important to me?
- What have I been afraid to start?

Potential

Adapted from Leonardo Da Vinci's *Vitruvian Man*, this is the first of two illustrations you'll find bookending this volume. I've diverted from the traditional Tarot deck to create a card that symbolises Potential. Here, you see a male figure and 22 sunrays – one for each chapter of this book – and the resulting burst of light signifies the release of your potential.

Be humble in your confidence yet courageous in your character.

- Melanie Koulouris

Chapter One
Self Confidence

Da Vinci

The little boy both lost and found himself. His bright and inquisitive little mind was completely absorbed in his task of gathering dead creepy crawlies of every kind: those that fly, crawl, have an exoskeleton, antennae, pincers, and many legs. The young lad then merely acted as the Latin origins of the word insect suggested. Insectum: cut into segments.

After dissecting them, he briefly studied the elements of their makeup. He then began to lose himself again, only this time to the imagination. He reconstructed the creatures using a variety of parts from other insects in a manner that was simultaneously visionary and disturbing.

Taking to paint brushes, with eagle-eyed attention to detail, he painted an image of his new creature. From the innocent collection of tiny, decomposing insects sprouted forth a spine-chilling, lively monster. He then handed his masterpiece over to his father who found the imagery of his son's imagination both terrifying and impressive. He also instinctively knew the finished piece would be valuable. So, rather than passing on the creation to the peasant who had commissioned the artwork in the first place, he elected to sell it to a notable Florentine art dealer. It was a wise choice. With the generous profit, he purchased a cheaper artwork decorated with a heart pierced by an arrow and gave that to the peasant, who was still pleased. Meanwhile, the Florentine art dealer sold the fire-breathing creation, born from the mind and efforts of a five-year-old, to the Duke of Milan.

The boy in question was Leonardo da Vinci, the ultimate Renaissance man. He's an excellent role model when it comes to the first step towards confidence: self-efficacy.

Self-efficacy is your belief in your ability to succeed. It includes being able to appreciate your value and then using that as a driving force for greatness. During his 67 years, Da Vinci became synonymous with the concept of being a robust and confident genius.

We can learn a lot from Leonardo's curiosity and super-human imagination. He mastered mathematics, engineering, literature, anatomy, astronomy, geology, cartography, palaeontology, writing, architecture, sculpting and, of course, painting. He even devised early concepts for tanks and parachutes. In fact, in the year 2000, Leonardo's parachute was tested. British skydiver, Adrian Nicholas, used Leonardo's sketches to build a parachute from canvas and wood and then leapt from a hot air balloon 3,000 metres over South Africa. While he made it most of the way using Leonardo's parachute, he was worried that the wooden structure would crush him upon landing so he cut himself free and used a regular parachute when he reached the 900-metre mark.

Leonardo faced much criticism in his life but remained steadfast in his values. Legend has it that he was a fastidious vegetarian and would even buy caged birds only to set them free once he got home. These kinds of values helped him craft a legacy that remains active today.

Another man who was steadfast and devoted to liberation was born 350 years after Leonardo died. Mahatma Gandhi, born in 1869, epitomises another primary consideration for improving self-confidence: self-esteem. Gandhi started out as a lawyer, challenging the status quo of human rights. He fought for the right to ride first class on a train, wear his turban, and even walk on the footpath. In 1906 he began his philosophy of Satyagraha – a word that loosely translates to "insistence on truth". He rallied Indian and Chinese communities to appeal the law that stated everyone from those two minorities must register and carry an identification card at all times. The concept of Satyagraha inspired the idea of non-violent protesting. Gandhi's life-long mission ultimately led to the independence of India from British Empiric Rule on the 15 August 1947.

What we can learn from da Vinci and Gandhi is that having the confidence to take actions based on morals, despite what others may think, will get you far. But don't get too carried away, you still need to be able to recognise when you take things too far, and you need to take ownership of your mistakes.

Gaining confidence, like any other personal improvement, comes from conscious application. Having confidence means you'll be able to inform, inspire and ignite confidence in others.

Birthday of the Unconquered Sun

When looking for a role model for success, Roman Emperor Aurelian is one to take into consideration. Born to humble beginnings around AD214, his professional journey began in the lower ranks of the military from where he competently rose to Officer, Commander, General, and finally, Emperor of Rome. During his reign as Emperor from AD 270-275, he played a vital role in putting an end to the long-standing period of military anarchy, civil wars, invasions, fragmentation, plagues and economic depression that was the Third Century.

In the short time that he held the title of Emperor, he defeated many tribes, including the Vandals (who, despite the suggestion of their name, actually conducted themselves better than many of the other barbaric tribes during the Sack of Rome). He commissioned the building of strong, sturdy walls that circled 19km around the Seven Hills of Rome to encompass and defend the area. Stretches of those steadfast Aurelian walls still stand today. He is credited with reuniting the separated Western and Eastern Roman Empires. Aurelian was also somewhat of a reformer: he offered free food, ensured stable prices for commodities that were required by all, and took a firm administrative stand to stamp out corruption among public officials.

Aurelian used his power to champion the beliefs that he held close to his heart, which is an admirable trait to consider when setting your goals. Closest to his heart was his family. Aurelian's mother is said to have been a high priestess of the Roman Empire's official sun deity, Sol Invictus, aka The Unconquered Sun.

Sol Invictus was so revered by Aurelian throughout his early life that when he became emperor, he formed an official cult and championed the celebratory festival Dies Natalis Solis Invicti or 'Birthday of The Unconquered Sun'.

Take a leaf from Aurelian's leadership book to adapt your contemporary version of Dies Natalis Solis Invicti. He has shown that if we strive to reach our goals while holding honourable and noble intentions, and acting with confidence (even forced and fake), we can lead meaningful and purposeful lives. Here are some guidelines:

- Move towards goals in which you hold a keen sense of desire; goals you're inclined to persevere with beyond a short-lived motivation
- Focus on goals that make your heart, eyes and mind burn brightly; goals which you know will deliver a sense of inner warmth
- Choose goals that, when accomplished, will shed a little more light on your life while simultaneously illuminating the lives of others
- Ultimately, work towards goals that encourage you and ignite your full potential
- Aspire to stamp out the vandals (saboteurs and naysayers) who would otherwise hold you back from your purpose
- Be steadfast and stalwart, like those Aurelian walls, and defend your vision
- Strive towards your objectives from a mindset of unity and collaboration, rather than division: 'me' turns to 'we', 'I' turns to 'us'
- Challenge the status quo from all ranks and stages of both your professional and personal life. Remember, you don't need to be an Emperor to tackle fragmented and broken systems or outdated societal limitations
- Be a disruptive reformer, but keep others in mind. Drive with passion and persistence towards accomplishments that are better for you, better for others, better for society as a whole, and better for the natural environment

The achievement of these goals is worthy of a Roman-style celebration – you've conquered your unconquerable sun.

Tarot: The Chariot

The Chariot card is a symbol of motivation and of overcoming challenges through confidence and control. By staying focussed on the task at hand and confident in your abilities, you can achieve your goals. You may even realise that striving towards your goal can be just as satisfying as attaining it.

In the traditional Tarot, the man sitting astride the chariot is adorned in a uniform that features crescent moons on the shoulders. These refer to the formative world – the outside influences that can shape our experiences, our opinions, our reactions, and the way in which we see the world. He tells us that we must withstand the rigours of what is required for us to achieve our goals. The card reminds us to assert ourselves and be bold in all that we do. We must be confident and vocal about our wants and needs; we must know what we want and what we stand for. Otherwise, we won't get anything we want. It also reminds us to keep an eye on our aggression – there is a fine line between aggression and confidence.

His uniform also features alchemical symbols that represent the spiritual transformation that we are all capable of once we understand how being determined, self-disciplined and hard-working can help us to overcome obstacles and make us stronger. Overall, the card demonstrates progress, growing in confidence, and a healthy respect for the self. The man holds no reins because he has no real hold over the chariot; only his strength of will can guide it in the right direction. There is usually a cityscape in the background to demonstrate that he has turned his back on civilisation to focus on the self.

Illustration:

An eagle, strong and proud, flies towards luminous Ra, the Sun God. Ancient Egyptians believed Ra to be the creator of the sky, the earth, and the underworld, and the eagle is often seen as the bird with the strongest connection to the divine because of the great heights it can reach. When you are confident and believe in yourself, you can reach greater heights.

Three quick tips:

- Regularly compliment others because how you view others is a reflection of how you view yourself
- Be more mindful of your posture and style. Our body language shows our internal state of mind
- Don't be shy to try positive affirmations beginning with "I am…" and following up with whatever it is you hope to achieve

Self-control is strength. Right thought is mastery. Calmness is power.

- James Allen

Chapter Two
Self-control

Bare bones of Emotional Intelligence

My first exposure to the German mentality of being naked in the sauna came in the form of a 16-year-old kid who grew up in the relatively quiet Scottish village of South Queensferry, just outside Edinburgh.

The man-sized teen was so large that I couldn't imagine the last time he would have been able to see his toes. He marched boldly, while completely naked, into the modest-sized sauna of the Forth Bridges Motel Fitness Centre. While I found it quite amusing, the other four patrons thought the ballsy move (pardon the pun) was entirely inappropriate. One old-school Scottish woman lashed out at the befuddled giant while another went to get backup. He ignored them and poured more water over the hot stones. Ignorance is bliss.

It took less than a minute for the on duty manager to intervene. Stepping fully suited into the sauna he hurriedly escorted the confused gentleman out of there by the elbow, trying to wrap a towel around him as they went. We listened as the manager sought to explain the difference between Scottish and German sauna etiquette, his voice fading as they walked down the hall.

I daresay he went on to explain that, while Scots may be famed for lack of underwear in public, there's still a heavy kilt to cover one's modesty. Any other such displays of bold nakedness would be kept to swift, rear view, cheeky flashes at sporting competitions where the foes are English.

Ten years later I was residing in the Austrian Tyrolean town of Hopfgarten where my steam room experience did a complete flip. I tried to remain cool, calm and collected in my Billabong boardies while everyone around me slouched around like Adam and Eve before they'd discovered the fig leaves.

So began a five-stage process of adapting to the towel-less Tyrolean environment.

Stage 1: Remove shorts but keep the towel wrapped and knotted firmly. Reveal partial thigh.

Stage 2: Loosen towel fully then drape to reveal an entire leg and thigh.

Stage 3: Strategically place towel on lap

Stage 4: Remove towel while leaning forward, then gradually sit upright for the final reveal.

Stage 5: Congratulations. You are naked.

You can, of course, skip stages 1-4 and proceed straight to stage five, as the locals do, given that ultimately the only element at play in such circumstances is your discomfort.

I share this short story as a quirky metaphor given it underpins a couple of fundamental lessons and reasons for applying all facets of Emotional Intelligence, with a focus on self-control.

Emotional Intelligence is the awareness, expression and control of your emotions, as well as the ability to handle relationships judiciously and empathetically. Being emotionally intelligent is to take the time to listen and understand a situation, and to judge people and things a little less swiftly.

Based on psychologist Daniel Goleman's model of Emotional Intelligence, here are five things to keep in mind:

Self-control

Learn to control or identify external circumstances that provoke you, remembering that nothing outside of yourself has the power to make you feel a certain way. Always take responsibility for all of your feelings and actions, especially when it comes to how you deal with and treat others. Ask yourself whether your response is appropriate because, after all, it's not what happens that is as important as how you choose to respond to it.

In the late '60s, Stanford University professor Walter Mischel conducted a voluntary restraint experiment with children aged 4-6 years old. A child was lead into a bare room with only a table and one chair. On the table was a marshmallow. The facilitator told the child that they could eat the treat immediately, or they could wait 15 minutes, and the treat would be doubled. The child was then left alone to battle with their self-control. Around a third of the participants managed to wait the full 15 minutes, with the other third scoffing the marshmallow as soon as they were left alone.

A fascinating aspect of the research came years later when the kids were assessed again. The data showed that those kids who were able to wait 15 minutes for greater reward were more attentive, skilful and socially adept than their greedy and impulsive counterparts.

They also performed better in their studies, proving that self-inflicted delayed gratification is a trait that can lead to smarter and more functional adults.

"You have power over your mind, not external events. Realise this, and you will find strength." – Marcus Aurelius

Self-awareness

Similar to self-control, self-awareness is the ability to recognise your emotional responses – the thoughts that trigger feelings and the behaviours that drive actions. Identify both your strengths and weaknesses, and then learn to leverage the former while managing the latter.

"Everything that irritates us about others can lead us to better understand ourselves." – Carl Jung

Motivation

Align your actions with your genuine intrinsic motivators – the things that motivate you out of real interest and ambition as opposed to being motivated by status and recognition. Make sure your thoughts, feelings and actions are taking you towards your goals. Leverage the principle of reframing: turn circumstances in your surrounding environment – positive or negative – to your advantage so that you stay focussed on your objectives. Collaborate your efforts and ensure win-win so others may also achieve their goals.

"If it's important to you, you will find a way. If not, you'll find an excuse." – Anon

Empathy

Endeavour to put yourself in other people's shoes. Are you aware of what is going on for them right now? Show genuine interest: ask questions, pay attention, listen, and then pause to digest what has been said before leaping to a conclusion. Look at the situation from a different perspective (visualising yourself as a fly on the wall or looking down from a helicopter is a good way to achieve this). Changing your perspective and accepting that there are reasons for other people's behaviours is a great starting point for learning to be a little less swift to judge someone.

"When people talk, listen completely. Most people never listen." – Ernest Hemingway

Social Skills

Think before you leap into action and focus on the quality of those actions. Be sure to communicate candidly and from a position of calmness (see Chapter 20), and treat others how you'd like to be treated in return. Make sure your words are aligned with your actions; never make empty promises or threats. Learn to be confident enough to make a stand for what you believe in while simultaneously respecting the rights and beliefs of others.

Any journey of adaptation and personal development may well make you feel a little uncomfortable. It might require an openness or vulnerability that perhaps also seems as if you're naked for the entire world to see. It's the application of Emotional Intelligence and awareness – of yourself and others – which helps to prevent potential upset or freak outs.

Those Scottish women could have expressed their dismay with less venom; the rotund, happy fellow could have sensed their discomfort, read their reactions, and realised something was amiss. If either party had sought first to understand the situation from the other's perspective rather than let habit determine their response, it would have been a more peaceful scenario.

Tarot: Temperance

The Temperance card features a winged angel with one foot on land (to represent the material world) and the other in the water (to represent the subconscious). The angel is advising us always to test the waters and show some self-control and discipline before jumping into unknown territory. The angel shows us how to be a temperate person who finds a balance between life's extremes while displaying qualities of truth, enthusiasm and tolerance. The path to success in achieving your goals is through harmony between desire and need.

Illustration:

The strong, calm, warrior woman demonstrates temperance. The flames surrounding her represent the emotional fluctuations that can interrupt your state of serenity. The warrior is patient, by having complete control of herself she can extinguish those destructive inner forces which would otherwise sabotage her calm.

Three quick tips

- Recognise where you are lacking in self-control and strive for improvement
- Look at your temptations objectively and they will no longer appear so alluring
- Eliminate the things that trigger pointless indulgence

Weakness of attitude becomes weakness of character.

- Albert Einstein

Chapter Three
Attitude

BRONZE and GOLD

In 1388, a lump of Belgian bronze was forged into a statue of a mischievous, naked little boy who was in the act of urinating into a fountain. The 24-inch figure was named Manneken Pis, which translates to "Little Man Pee in Marols".

There are many great legends and myths concerning the origins of the sculpture. Perhaps it's a representation of a 12th Century infant royal, who, to encourage his country's troops, was put in a basket and hung from a tree. Legend has it that he showered his contempt for the attacking front line by urinating on the foes from his princely perch. His country's victory in that battle could very possibly be attributed to the baby's bladder bravado.

A more likely story is that of medieval Brussels being under siege. Attackers apparently tried to blow down the city walls with explosives, but they were no match for a small boy with a small bladder. He urinated on the dangerous fuses and thus prevented the municipal from being parched to an ember.

Regardless of which anecdote appeals to the raconteur in you, this little statue has a mighty presence in Brussels. The locals adorn their peeing, cheeky cherub in extravagant costumes so that he doesn't need to urinate in the buff. It gets pretty cold in Brussels.

Jump forward some 570 years, and you'll find that the act of men of short stature peeing in the face of the enemy is not just reserved for those who lived in the 12th Century. Hollywood hunk James Dean (who stood at a mere 173cm tall) allegedly took a leak on the set of *Giant* while filming his first scene with Elizabeth Taylor. He casually swaggered back to his position and nailed the scene in one take, and when Dennis Hopper asked him why he made such a bold move, he replied: "Well, I was really nervous. I figured if I could go and pee in front of all those people I could do anything on film."

Where Manneken Pis urinated on his physical enemies, James Dean urinated on his mental ones. For the record, I'm not condoning urinating in public in a desperate attempt to defeat your enemies (mental or otherwise), but the confident attitude that it takes to do something so daring is to be admired.

What I'd like you to take away from these two anecdotes is this: If a 24-year old actor or a 24-inch sculpture of a toddler can inspire such respect and admiration for such a daring act, what could you achieve with the same attitude? Take a leaf out of the Manneken Pis book and cast your attitude out of BRONZE.

Brave

Respectful

Optimistic

Noble

Zealous

Effervescent

Or upgrade to cast it out of GOLD

Good to others

Open-minded

Love yourself

Display composure

As you can see, the first step towards conquering your enemies – whether they are human or just enemies to your productivity; anything that is determined to derail you – is to change your attitude towards them. Once you conquer your enemies, you can do anything. Attitude is everything.

Like the clothes you wear and the food you eat, attitude is something you get to choose every day. What's more, your choice of attitude also can nourish you and can command a greater first impression than any designer outfit. A fantastic temperament can mesmerise others, while a terrible tantrum will turn people away.

The key here is not to take yourself too seriously. Indulge in hilarity. As poet and novelist May Sarton says, "Each day, and the living of it has to be a conscious creation in which discipline and order are relieved with some play and pure foolishness." Such a lovely reminder, that "It's not what happens that's important, it's how you choose to respond."

Tarot: The Sun

The sun begins the dawn that follows the darkest night. It is a guiding beacon for positivity and fulfilment, representing the source of life itself. On some cards, you'll see a naked child (think of Manneken Pis) basking joyfully in the sunshine and reminding us that we are at our happiest when we are authentic. The white horse represents resilience and the coloured flags in the child's hands show how control can be passed from the conscious to the subconscious. If we are determined enough, we can turn the BRONZE elements into gold ones that become innate qualities, second-nature traits that can improve our lives. The Sun radiates inspiration, insight and energy. It makes us feel alive.

Illustration:

Linked closely to a natural inner confidence, the theme of the eagle continues. It has now reached the bright sun and grasps it firmly in its talons, symbolic of the attitude the eagle will carry forth to shine on others. A hint of the *Vitruvian Man* represents the balance between an ideal demeanour, a tranquil heart, and unbiased perspective.

Three quick tips

- Kick-start each day with something positive
- Seek out people who inspire and encourage you
- Be polite

Reading is to the mind what exercise is to the body.

- Joseph Addison

Chapter Four
Wellness

We're all made from stars: body, mind, and spirit potential

The next time you hit a wall, take stock of what you're made of and what that means you're capable of doing.

According to Carl Sagan (and Moby), we are all made from stars.

The night sky is made up of 100 billion stars, and the average human is made up of seven billion billion billion atoms. It's mind boggling to think that they could have formed at the same time during the Big Bang 13.8 billion years ago. The carbon, nitrogen, oxygen and other heavy elements that exist within you probably came from nebulae (the clouds of swirling gases) and forged from the embers of supernova (dying stars).

Your heart will pump nearly one million barrels of blood during your lifetime – that's 800 million pints of beer – and it beats around 100,000 times every day, creating the same amount of energy it takes to drive a truck 32 kilometres.

Everyone knows the five traditional senses of smell, sight, sound, touch and taste, but did you know just how complex they are? When it comes to smell, you have the ability to detect one trillion different odours. And sight? Each of your eyes contains over two million moving parts and can distinguish around 2.7 million colours. Your eyes are so sensitive that if the earth was flat and you had 20-20 vision, you'd be able to see a candle flickering 48 kilometres away. What about touch? The human finger can feel objects as small as 13 nanometres, meaning that if your finger were the size of the earth, you'd be able to feel the spaces between houses and cars. And taste? Your tongue has around 10,000 taste buds that are replaced every two weeks.

Many neurologists have identified an additional four senses, while others believe there could be as many as 16 more. These include balance, proprioception (knowing where your body parts are in relation to other body parts), thirst, hunger, and time.

Human bones, ounce for ounce, are stronger than steel. Even your muscles are far stronger than they appear. Physical strength is limited to protect the tendons and muscles from hurting themselves, but the limitation can be lifted during a mad rush of adrenaline, like when you hear of mothers being able to pick up cars and buses when their child is trapped. The iron in your body, if fused together, could be moulded into a three-inch nail. Even a strand of hair can support 100 grams of weight, while a full head of hair can support up to 12 tonnes, equal to the weight of two elephants. And given our upright posture, humans are the best adapted and most developed long-distance runners in the animal kingdom. So if you turn into a couch potato, you deny who you are at your core.

If the brain were a computer, it could perform 38 thousand trillion operations per second at full efficiency. In a lifetime your brain's long-term memory can hold as much as one quadrillion separate bits of information. Your brain scans a lifetime of experiences hundreds of times swifter than the efficiency of the most advanced technology available, all of which happens quicker than the blink of an eye.

Your brain's 100 billion neurones are on a par with the number of the stars in the galaxy. Your brain may only be 2% of your total body weight, but it uses 25% of your body's nutrients to properly function. In doing so, your brain generates more electrical impulses in a single day than all the phones in the world combined.

It's said the average weight of the human brain is 1.4kg, yet Albert Einstein's weighed around 1.2kg, proving, after all, that size doesn't matter. The average mind is said to generate between 50,000-70,000 thoughts a day, so when you learn to filter the best of them, you'll boost up a gear. What's more, your brain manages all of the above, and far more, only channelling the equivalent of 20 watts of power. Which, to put into context, is the amount required to power a single light globe.

No living architect, scientist, or engineer could blueprint, map or build you. You are more finely engineered than any top-end technology, and you are more delicate and precise than even the most finely designed Swiss watch.

So, the next time you hit a brick wall, remember what you're made of and what you're capable of, and smash right through it! While the dollar value of the chemical components in your body may only add up to only a few hundred dollars, the manner in which they function makes you truly priceless.

It doesn't matter if you're not ripped or buff. It doesn't matter if you're not scoring as a genius on the IQ scale. You are luminous – like a starburst – because you are bioluminescent. Yes, you glow in the dark. But, as advanced as human sight is, the light is too weak for the naked eye to detect.

Besides, you were the quickest of 100 million sperm, so you're already a winner. You have the potential and ability to create your big bang of infinite possibilities.

Take care of your body and your body will, to the best of its ability, return the favour. You become fit in the gym and lose weight in the kitchen, yet your overall wellness comes from the level of conscious control you have over your headspace. In the words of the Dalai Lama, "Happiness can be achieved through the training of the mind."

Human beings are capable of incredible things when they put their minds to it.

Usain Bolt ran 100 metres in 9.58 seconds.

Cate Campbell swam 100 metres in 50.91 seconds.

Mike Powell landed 8.95 metres away in long jump.

Alan Eustace jumped from 135,980 feet with a parachute, while Red Bull's Felix Baumgartner holds the record for the longest and fastest freefall at 4 minutes and 20 seconds, making him the first person to break the sound barrier outside of a moving vehicle.

Nuno Gomes dove to a depth of 318.25 metres, while Aleix Vendrell held his breath underwater for a seemingly impossible 24 minutes and 3 seconds.

Sherpas Phurba Tashi and Apa Sherpa have made it to the top of Mount Everest 21 times. The oldest person to make it to the top was 80, and the youngest 13.

These feats of strength and endurance are but a drop in the ocean of human endeavours. The human body is an amazing machine – it can run, swim, jump, dive, and climb – and we can train it to reach its full potential.

During my studies, I've come to realise that natural therapies, headspace, exercise and nutrition are as important as each other. While we understand how the connection between the mind and the body can be an important tool when it comes to visualisation and training, little is understood about our consciousness, which means we could be capable of far more than we realise. Where our science is now will no doubt seem like child's play in 500 years, but I'm pretty comfortable with what we know so far: that performance and potential can be tapped into by investing in both the mind and body.

Tarot: Star

The traditional Star card shows a naked woman holding two containers by the edge of a pool. She pours water from one container into five rivulets, representative of the five senses. The Star card reminds us that the universe has blessed us - we already have all the courage and fulfilment we need, we just need to tune into it. The Star is an important card regarding personal transformation - it tells us to be open to new ideas and growth. It's an encouraging card, especially if you've been through a rough patch or have experienced setbacks.

Illustration:

The central figure is the epitome of wellness. *The Book of Knowledge* and the lotus flower indicate total wellness of body, mind and spirit. An intricate pattern weaved throughout captures the idea that a consistent approach is required to maintain this overall balance. The figure's third eye, wide open in the shape of a celestial body, is a reminder of the amazing possibilities that exist within you.

Three quick tips:

- Enjoy a balanced lifestyle that takes both your physical and mental health into account
- Be sure to nourish your mind, body and spirit
- Spend some time alone in silent meditation, in nature, or out on an adventure

Realise deeply that the present moment is all you ever have. Make the Now the primary focus of your life.

- Eckhart Tolle

Chapter Five
Present

Excess baggage

Given my life and career have revolved much around travelling, it's to be expected that I have my fair share of baggage. In fact, we all do. The next time you go on a trip, take stock of your luggage. If your physical luggage is lighter than your mental baggage, it's time to take a step back.

Your biggest suitcase is the physical equivalent to your heaviest emotional baggage – it's the hardest stuff to lug around and the stuff you're keen to ditch soonest at the airport check-in. When it comes to the contents of this suitcase, how much of it do you actually need? The third pair of shoes? That bikini? That little embarrassing moment from 1997? The memories of your first heartbreak? Take the time to unpack and repack mentally. What can you leave behind? Better yet, what can you throw away? Stop carting all that excess baggage around.

Then there's the backpack. Full of our daily gripes, we wear it over our shoulders and carry it around from the moment we leave the house until we get home. Unzip your metaphorical backpack and throw away the rubbish you've collected, like those little disagreements and disputes that don't really matter in the grand scheme of things. They're not worth ruining your posture over.

If you're going on a beach trip, you're probably going to have a beach ball somewhere in your luggage. Think of the beach ball as the gossip that gets passed around from person to person. Even if what they're saying isn't true, people love to get involved and kick the ball around with everyone else. So, next time you find yourself extending a leg to kick the ball, so to speak, ask yourself if what you're getting involved in is necessary and kind. If not, let the ball sail right past you. Or better yet, deflate it.

If you're a conscientious packer, you'll no doubt have a first aid kid. This holds all our health concerns, both real and imagined. Lighten your load by resisting the temptation to google your symptoms – it only adds anxiety. If you're genuinely worried, see a doctor. If not, just enjoy your health.

Lastly, if you're travelling with kids, you'll most likely have some of their toys with you – maybe a magic eight ball. We have a tendency to try to predict the future by over analysing and over thinking things to the point where we're worried about something that hasn't happened yet (and probably won't happen, to be honest). This is the mental equivalent of carrying around a giant magic eight ball – it's unreliable, inconvenient to carry, and it never gives you the answer you want. Leave it behind.

It's important to realise that not all baggage is negative. It's part of life – we live, and we collect experiences and memories, some of which we never want to let go. It's when the baggage impedes on the present moment and inhibits our movements that we need to rethink what we're carrying and why.

Take some time for self-reflection. Ultimately, it's up to you what you carry around. You can choose to travel light by living with acceptance, gratitude and patience. The impact something has on you is in your direct control. You can do something about it now, or throw it in the suitcase to lug around and deal with later, if ever. You owe it to yourself to make your life as comfortable and enjoyable as possible.

Tarot: Death

The Death card is, by far, the most misunderstood card in the Tarot deck. It's not a card to be taken literally! It can actually be one of the most positive cards to draw. The card shows the figure of Death - a skeleton holding a black and white flag - riding a horse and wearing armour that indicates he is invincible. The horse represents purity, and the white rose shows beauty. The sun signifies immortality because the sun appears to die every night, only to rise again every morning. Drawing the Death card means that a major phase of your life has come to an end, and new beginnings are on their way. You need to put the past behind you to actually appreciate these new opportunities, even though you might experience pain and discomfort in the process. The card signifies a time of transformation and change. It tells you that you need to clear some space in your life for new experiences.

Illustration:

The most obvious symbol for the ability to live in the moment is a clock. It creates a path that winds and weaves into the future, from the present, trailing backwards into the past. The power of Now is represented by a bright ruby; a significant reminder of how precious each moment is. The Future spirals into the gaping hollowed sleeves of the anonymous figure, and in doing so, enters a dark cavern that represents the unknown.

Three quick tips:

- Take note of how often you think about the past and the future, and compare it to how often you're in the moment.
- It's okay just to do nothing sometimes. You don't need to feel obligated to say yes to everything.
- Eliminate physical clutter and purge yourself of unnecessary possessions.

If you're looking for that one thing that will change your life, look in a mirror.

- Unknown

Chapter Six
Self Reflection

Behavioural sciences: six thinking hacks

Like it or not, the word 'selfie' has found a place in the Oxford Dictionary. In fact, it was even word of the year in 2013, which isn't surprising given that up to 80 million photos are posted on Instagram every day, with some sources saying that the hashtag 'selfie' features on around 8% of those. While Millennials are expected to take over 25,000 selfies in their lifetime, the concept of the selfie is nothing new. The first official selfie was taken by and of Robert Cornelius in 1839 when he was accidentally snapped while testing the light for a photoshoot.

Some people laugh at the idea of the modern day selfie – calling the people who take them insecure or narcissistic. Lexi Herrick's article *The 11 Things We Fake in Our Social Media Lives* takes the selfie hate one step further, saying:

> *It's this kind of distortion that only serves to sabotage our ability for honest self-reflection. Suddenly it seems to matter less whether we are in good or bad shape, healthy, wealthy, or happy, as long as we look good and pick a good filter. But we don't have to give into the social media selfie culture. Like anything else in life, we can choose how much it impacts us and infiltrates our day-to-day lives.*

It might serve us better to stop hashtagging #selfie and start hashtagging #selfreflection.

Honest self-reflection can be tough; it means going deeper than the surface to see what's behind those scars and wrinkles. It means realising that good-looking people can have ugly hearts, and vice versa.

Everyone has off days. We melt down, and we get frustrated, and we feel inferior. The way we feel on the inside is usually what impacts our external environment, and when this is reflected back to us, we blame the rest of the world for causing our pain and confusion.

Here are six Jedi mind tricks that you can perform on yourself when you need to get your head back in the game.

1: Flip the switch

Internal dialogue – the soul's soliloquy – is normal. While a dose of self-criticism can be constructive, the sabotaging inner voice often takes things too far. Studies show that the majority of our internal talk is negative. Ask yourself, how long would you keep a friend who only berated and insulted you every time you met? Probably not long.

We can all agree Einstein knew a thing or two about problem-solving. He worked on the premise that the more time you spend trying to understand and define the problem, the better the solution. He also worked on the supposition that no problem can ever be solved on the same level of consciousness from which it was created. In simpler words: Flip the switch from negative self-talk to quality, constructive questions.

If you find yourself listing reasons as to why something can't be achieved, flip the switch and ask yourself: what will it take to get this done?

If you find yourself trying the same solutions over and over, and failing each time, flip the switch and ask yourself: what haven't I tried yet?

The quality of your internal questions determines whether you're incessantly chewing on problems as if they're a piece of gum, or contemplating how to reach a level of consciousness where solutions lie. (Hint: it doesn't involve intoxication.)

2: Control vs. influence

Unfortunately, we don't live in a world where we can snap our fingers and get what we want when we want it. Instead of trying to change things through the sheer power of will, realise that you can take real action and assert real influence on your circumstances and while it's impossible to control other people, it is possible to control yourself (see Chapter Two). Once we are in control of ourselves, we can begin to influence others. Try to focus on the following:

- Ask yourself: what can I directly control?
- Ask yourself: what do I have influence over, and what kind of influence is it?
- Recognise there are facets to every situation that are beyond your control. The sooner you accept this, the sooner you will be free from the burden. Think of the prayer of serenity: "Grant to us the serenity of mind to accept that which cannot be changed; courage to change that which can be changed, and wisdom to know the one from the other."

3: Manage emotions

While it may feel good to smash out an angry email to your boss with no intention of sending it (praise be to the 'undo send' button), it's more important to learn how to manage your emotions. Plus you've only got 30 seconds to click 'undo'.

Don't mistake emotions for passion because often when emotions are heightened, intelligence is pushed to the background. Passion should drive your decisions while emotions should not. This is where the concept of mindfulness comes into play. The ability to recognise and manage your emotions can guide your thinking and behaviour. There's a time and place for emotional outbursts (you can howl and thump your chest as much as you like at a football grand final), but the workplace isn't one of them.

4: Mood impacts momentum

I respect the principle of meditation (see Chapter 11), though it's not as easy as it sounds to silence your mind. And for the record, passing out or falling asleep doesn't count as reaching enlightenment.

Mindfulness is a kind of meditation that may sound counter-intuitive to the traditional practice of focussing on your breath in order to still your mind. Mindfulness allows you to follow your thoughts rather than fighting them into submission, so you can achieve peace.

Rather than letting your thoughts influence your mood and your feelings impact your actions, find a way to live harmoniously with them. Once you are in harmony with your mind, you will have a clear path to success with no internal roadblocks. Remember, feelings are just like visitors. Let them come and go.

5: Creative think-tank

"Logic will get you from A to Z. Imagination will get you everywhere." - Albert Einstein.

"Pure logic is the ruin of spirit." - Antoine de Saint-Exupéry

The underpinning principle of behavioural science is that all human beings are wired to base their decisions on logic and emotion. Next time you find yourself stuck, step out of emotion and logic and into creativity. Creative thinking is a valid and powerful way to re-ignite your mojo. Try to find a creative outlet that awakens your playful side, like finger painting, DIYing, or raking leaves and then jumping into the pile.

6: Face the mirror

The world is bigger than we think it is. Other people impact us all the time, even if we can't feel or see it. Sometimes it's for the best, and other times they let us down, but either way, it's important not to play the blame game. We can't avoid personal responsibility, so this last hack is designed to keep you honest. So, before you point the finger of blame, be sure to face the mirror first and ask yourself: what part of the situation can you control? In every situation there is some part – however small – that is yours to own, so own it.

Tarot: Justice

The most important aspect of the Justice card, for us, is the notion of cause and effect. We are reminded to take a rational, unbiased view of the situation, and to look logically and objectively at it, and ourselves. We must strive to find the whole truth, even if it means accepting responsibility for our mistakes.

The figure of justice holds a sword in her right hand and scales in her left. The square on her crown represents well-ordered thoughts. The clasp on her cloak is made up of a square and a circle – the square protects the circle and the eternal state of oneness we are all capable of reaching. The sword signifies victory, logic, and a well-ordered mindset. The scales she holds in her left hand – the intuitive hand – show that logic must be based on instinct.

Illustration:

A butterfly, seen from a side perspective, casts a reflection in a watery mirror, symbolising individual flow. The vibrant colour is a reminder that external beauty exists and radiates to its fullest when met with intrinsic light. The Scales of Justice feature quietly in the background as a nod to the traditional Tarot and a reminder that balanced judgement comes from the truth.

Three quick tips:

- Seek and encourage honest feedback
- Consider studying a behavioural science (EQ, DISC, WPMot) to help identify your values, skills and abilities
- Look at the situation from a different perspective

There are two primary choices in life: to accept conditions as they exist, or accept the responsibility for changing them.

- Denis Waitley

Chapter Seven
Tonics

Burgers and Brussels sprouts: metaphors for universal toxins and tonics

McDonald's Restaurant Hazeldonk:
Dutch-Belgian border:
9am, September 1995

After two days of Dutch debauchery, countless temptations, indulgences, diversions and delusions caused by the bewitching allure of Amsterdam's alleyways, the pandemonium begins.

Food orders are shouted from all directions, landing on a solitary stranger. Thanks to two coach loads of 18-30 year-old sightseers who've just arrived with the mid-morning munchies, being in this fast food outlet feels more like standing on a stock exchange floor.

The after-effects of drinking games (such as those whereupon a spinning dildo divines who will take the next shot), drugs, and close encounters of the Red Light kind have taken their toll, leaving everyone with the kind of hangover that only fast, fat food can cure.

The Belgian or Dutch cashier (it's hard to pinpoint exactly which as he is barely audible amidst the cacophony, so we'll call him Butch) stands as a lone guard. His register is the only available gateway for guests to place their gluttonous orders. The chaos would be almost bearable if it weren't for the other 100-plus like-minded tourists fighting it out for top ordering position in the front row. The horde is three-deep, barging against each other in an attempt to crush their hunger with legendary, Golden Arch gastronomic delights.

The flow of food orders pouring through this single open register threatens to swamp the cooking crew, yet they seem oblivious to the swift decline in their patrons' already-minimal patience. One girl looks confused as she flips fillings into buns in an otherwise empty kitchen, and the only other staffer in sight is a lethargic, androgynous teenager whose only apparent job involves shovelling fries into boxes at a snail's pace. I'm sure there are other competent McPersonnel floating around somewhere, but given the surprise arrival of the ravenous revellers, they're probably reluctant to come out of hiding.

The visible team members share seven gold stars between them: three of which belong to Butch, and none of which seem to accurately reflect their ability to deal with hungry, holidaying hordes. Regardless, the rush for value meals is well and truly on, and the 'quick service' upon which this world-leading franchise prides itself is fast becoming as mythical to me as Ronald's healthy eating options.

Amongst the madness, one hung-over Aussie throws a curve ball at the cashier, a simple request that was about to take this ship from sinking to McSunk: "One Big Mac Meal!"

Butch attempts to define, in broken English, that Ronald has implemented strict laws that govern when certain meals are available to diners: "Ah, dish-is-not-poshible-cosh-we're-shtill-sherving-on-de-Breakfasht-Menu."

In this, the most liberal of European nations, you'd think ordering a Big Mac before 10:30 would be permitted, probably even served with a kiss from the chef and smokable French fries. The bleary eyed, country boy from outback Oz is hardly an uptown food critic: only two nights ago he was on a Red Light stage taking bites out of a banana that had been wedged up against a stripper's vagina. Yet, as a conventional connoisseur of convenience cooking, he manages to sum up the mood of the omnivorous mob in four words: "What a flamin' kroc!" (I'm pretty sure he doesn't mean it as a cheery praise for this franchise's founder, Ray Kroc.)

I vaguely remember researching (on the back of a chip packet or some equally ridiculous reference source) that McDonald's has well over thirty-thousand restaurants worldwide, with a combined output of more than forty-six million satisfied customers daily. It doesn't take long for Ronald and his McCalculator to theorise that he's lobbing out a Happy Meal somewhere in the world every smidgeon of a second. This particular Hazeldonk branch must have been excluded from statistics relating to any such speed or competence survey.

It's while observing the McMadness from the uncomfortable sidelines that I'm exposed to a familiar question from a bored patron: "Excuse me Mark, I know we're close to Belgium, I just wanted to know if that's where Brussels sprouts come from?" I know he cares more about killing time than getting an actual answer, but I'd been asked this question so often I finally decided to seek out a real answer rather than give another a fictitious response.

As it happens, the tiny green cabbage-related vegetables are indeed Belgian in origin. Their roots first spread to England, then to France, and finally to 1920s sunny California. Like many other wannabe icons, their plantings in the USA allowed them to break into the mainstream. I daresay there are still pockets of indigenous tribes, perhaps in the Amazon Basin, Darkest Africa or wildest areas of Wisconsin, who instantly recognise the mighty Golden Arches, but are yet to discover the aromatic delights that come from boiling hardy little Belgian sprouts.

I'm still amazed by the number of people exercising food prejudice and refusing to give sprouts access to a dinner plate. Should a clever sprout ever commit vegetable espionage and infiltrate a meal under guise of its first cousin Broccoli, it can expect nothing short of disgusted eviction. The universal dislike for this vegetable seems suddenly strange when you discover how fantastically nutritious the little odour bombs actually are. Did you know an average serve of three-and-a-half ounces of Brussels sprouts delivers about 140% of the recommended daily Vitamin C intake? You'll also benefit from an abundance of Vitamins A, B, E and Fe26 (Iron). A further chemical perquisite, notably potassium, works to cure your hangover and get rid of that horrible furry feeling in your mouth. You could speculate then that sprouts are an ideal, natural way to expunge all remnants of your Dutch debauchery, and something that would calm the Golden Arch of madness taking place all around.

Imagine if there was a healthy eating option next to every fast food joint, one that offered superior sources of nourishment, including the mini, green Brussels champions. Do you think people would choose to eat there? No. They almost never would – myself included. This is not a dig at convenient food chains (hell, even Contiki brochures used to feature the line 'See if you can out drink your driver!' as a unique selling point). Most food franchises have made a conscious shift towards healthier eating options since the Hazeldonk McFiasco of the mid '90s. Times change and every business consciously alters its product to throw in a side of social responsibility and philanthropy.

Sitting in the confines of that Hazeldonk restaurant watching the morning McMadness unfold around me, I answered a pretty dull question about vegetables, but my neurons fired up and I was left thinking about toxins and tonics. I came to the realisation that there is much more to our cravings than good or bad food choices: it's a question of holistic, essential sustenance for the body and mind.

Burgers and Brussels sprouts are merely metaphors for the way we sustain our larger, more existential needs. Maslow's Hierarchy of Needs offers a good breakdown of what those are:

- Physiological: breathing, food, water, sex, sleep, basic survival
- Security: of body, employment, resources, morality, family, health
- Love and belonging: friendship, family, intimacy
- Self-esteem: confidence, achievement, respect for and from others
- Self-actualisation: morality, creativity, spontaneity, problem solving

Sometimes it's easy to hold onto what we know to be septic, simply because it's convenient, habitual or cheap, but there are always smarter and bolder moves that can be made. Personify the tonics and toxins in all aspects of your life and make a conscious decision to surround yourself with the best situations and people. Flush the perfunctory, or just plain nasty, toxic ones out. Each day gives us possibilities to make new choices, and to give Brussels sprouts a chance.

Tarot: Devil

The Devil is presented as a half-man, half-goat hybrid creature. The man is considered to be unclean and lustful, while the goat symbolises the scapegoat, or the person or thing upon which we project our inferiorities in order to make ourselves feel better. The Devil's vampire bat wings are symbolic of what happens when we give in to our raw desires (it sucks the life blood from us, causing us to lose our vitality and energy). Look to the Devil card and you'll see a man and woman who are chained, seemingly against their will, but look closer again and you'll see that their shackles could be easily removed. This is significant of the fears, beliefs or situations you find yourself in that you may not realise are unhealthy for you.

Illustration:

We see a magnificent, detailed close-up of the wolf: capturing an ancient Indian proverb about the battle of choices that lives within us all. In this instance, the wolf's eye shimmers as it ponders its current state, reflecting the duality of our good and bad choices. The contradictory forces of dark and light are highlighted in the yin and yang.

Three quick tips:

- Establish and then maintain healthy boundaries with others
- Take personal responsibility and accountability for your mistakes
- Always be willing to make a stand for what you believe in

Successful people make decisions quickly (as soon as all the facts are available) and change them very slowly (if ever).

Unsuccessful people make decisions very slowly, and change them often and quickly.

- Napoleon Hill

Chapter Eight
Decisions

The First Day Talk

It's been the length of time it takes to grow Gandalf's beard since I last delivered the Contiki tour leader's First Day Talk. The speech takes place during the drive from London to the Port of Dover and is the first opportunity to set the tone and expectations for the whole trip, be it seven nights or seven weeks.

I'd spend many days passionately invested in study, committing a plethora of French history to memory to wow passengers with during an illuminating, slow-paced drive through Paris on their first night in continental Europe. But all of that was a walk in the park compared to the First Day Talk.

When you lead thousands of people, from every corner of the globe across multiple countries, you learn that almost every element of a tour may be in your sphere of influence, yet never entirely in your control.

It's been 14 years since I last sat in the bloody uncomfortable chair that is the tour guide's jump seat, but the three boundaries I used to inspire harmony on board are still relevant in other areas of life.

My three golden rules have been translated in the safe sanctuary of learning environments, across countless meeting rooms, and through keynote presentations in 47 countries. From first-hand experience in Europe, Asia-Pacific, South Africa and America, I've found these three rules transgress even the boundaries of geography or culture.

Rule 1: It's your fault if you get left behind

Be accountable for your actions. Even if you have a tour guide or manager to support you, you must ultimately take responsibility for yourself. If you are a leader, encourage accountability in your direct reports.

Rule 2: Candid conversations can solve just about any issue

Despite the constant propaganda that all tour brochures promise, the sun may not be shining the day you're banking on swimming at a Cannes beach, and scaffolding will almost certainly photo bomb your otherwise perfect happy-snaps of Europe's top attractions. And not everyone on your tour will be someone you would naturally choose to socialise with back home. In fact, often the opposite is true.

Resolving personality clashes, or even breaking up physical fights, comes with the turf as a tour leader. In fact, I learnt more about the psychology of human behaviour while on a Contiki coach, than in the hands-on application of tools such as the Myers–Briggs Type Indicator (MBTI) or Emotional Intelligence (EQ).

While you're leading a group of 50 people, all of whom have different expectations, it's inevitable some of them won't agree with the decisions you make. And that's okay. Decisions have to be made for the greater good.

The only way you could expect a resolution of any kind to something that's not working for you is through, direct, honest, open conversation and a willingness to also listen and respect a different perspective. (See Chapter 20.)

Encourage an environment where views are respected, and conflicts are resolved through collaboration and candour: swiftly, without the loss of productivity or the creation of additional stress.

Rule 3: Keep it together

Irritating minor discontents (actually the harshest derailer for harmony on a coach tour), inevitable delays, and even disasters (including the worst kind: client deaths) are potentially just around the corner.

When you're the leader, you're required to hold everything together when the proverbial hits the fan.

As a tour guide, if you can name it, you will probably have to deal with it. A dozen hours stuck in traffic in the middle of winter, 12-hour border crossings from Russia back to Western Europe, missed ferries, lost passports, being separated in Rome, and even having three passengers get run over by the same car in Venice.

In dealing with so many scenarios, I learnt that handling emotionally charged disaster is no different to managing niggling disdain due to minor discontents (where no lives were at risk). People tend to get behind you more when you're trying your best to deal with chaos. When something breaks, as a leader you can expect the finger of blame to be pointed in your direction, whether you deserve it or not.

And if you're a finger pointer, please remember next time your train or plane is delayed. I doubt the staff does it deliberately, so they could probably do without the aggression.

There are ups and downs ahead of you and your team. The sooner you grasp the concept that calmness is power, you'll be able to lead more confidently.

Decision-making and leadership go hand in hand. And this is where the second principle of the First Day Talk comes in. In making choices for a group of 50 people, you learn you can't please everyone all the time. Learning to lead through influence, along with an open-door policy and candid conversation, means that everyone can at least freely seek to understand why choices are being made.

As CEO of your life, leader of your destiny, and creator of your luck, mastering the ability to make wise decisions is an important tool for fulfilment and peak performance. Mastering decision-making in conjunction with recognising tonics (see Chapter Seven) and learning how to conduct honest self-reflection (see Chapter Six) will see you grow mature as a leader.

We make multiple decisions every day, from the simple to complex. What to wear, what to eat for breakfast, what coffee to have, when to eat lunch, and what time to go to the gym, or whether to go to the gym at all, to name just a few.

Be mindful of decision-making as an energy consuming process. Studies show that judges deciding on parole hearings make less favourable sentences later in a day or after long sessions because they suffer from decision-making fatigue.

Signs you may be suffering from decision fatigue include putting off making decisions altogether or making rash decisions.

Decision fatigue shows itself in multiple ways like procrastination, indecisiveness, impulsiveness, over-thinking or even complete avoidance.

It's no coincidence that people like Steve Jobs and Mark Zuckerberg are known for wearing the same simple outfits over and over. Why expend valuable time and energy on the less important decisions? Time is your most precious commodity

You can be well equipped to make critical choices in your life if you follow some fundamental principles for better decision-making:

- While it's possible not to do enough research, it's also possible to do too much
- While it's possible to be too emotional about a decision, it's also possible to not be emotional enough
- While it's possible to seek too much input from others, it's also possible not to seek enough

Israeli-American psychologist Daniel Kahneman has written many books and papers in empirical findings on the field of judgement and decision-making. In 2002 he was awarded a Nobel Prize for this work. Even the most analytical of people may have already made an emotional decision at a subconscious level. As Kahneman puts it, "We think, each of us, that we're much more rational than we are. And we think that we make our decisions because we have good reasons to make them. Even when it's the other way around. We believe in the reasons because we've already made the decision."

That said, a healthy balance of reasoning on top of the subconscious decision you've already made never goes amiss. When it comes to peak performance decision-making, logic and heart both play a part. Trust your natural rhythm, flow and balance as you leverage these two levers.

Tarot: Judgement

This card shows many naked men, women and children waiting to be judged by the archangel Gabriel. The card calls for reflection and self-evaluation as you make important decisions about your future. You may have come to a point where you understand the common themes of your life and now need to find a way to avoid or change them. You may have also had an epiphany where you have seen that you need to live your life differently by making better decisions, or by treating others differently. Drawing this card signifies that you have evaluated your past experiences, learnt from them, and are well equipped to make better decisions in the future.

Illustration:

The maze reflects the complex nature of the brain. The lightning bolt fires it into action so it can receive, filter and analyse millions of bits of information in the blink of an eye. Complex equations represent the analytical side of the brain, while explosions of hearts capture the emotional and creative side.

Three quick tips:

- Disregard your ego and excess emotion when you're making a decision
- Ensure that you have sufficient information and advice from reliable sources
- Avoid over-thinking so that you don't suffer from decision-making fatigue

The secret of change is to focus all of your energy, not on fighting the old, but on building the new.

- Dan Millman

Chapter Nine
Adaptability

A set of directions for personal development

To prepare a tour director for their first trip across Europe is akin to cramming a bachelor's degree in history into two months.

To be considered credible, trainees have to learn directions, histories, routes, tourist information, site-specific hot spots and festivals, along with a superabundance of general local knowledge – everything from the price of a cup of coffee to cultural nuances and differences.

There are also corporate functions of the role which entail financial management, and operational logistics, both of which, back in the '90s, included dealing with more currencies, fewer open borders, and more visa complexities.

On top of all that, they must have leadership capabilities and the ability to respond to a crisis. When leading thousands of guests across thousands of kilometres, the nature of probability means that even the best-laid plans will be derailed once in a while.

After the initial training, the tour director will be thrown into a bus with 50 paying guests. Each passenger has saved around $20,000 to secure that seat (when you consider flights, tour costs and general spending money), so, as a first-time tour director you're faced with a combined investment of about $1 million. Any significant amount of money comes with high expectations: "Give me a great trip. The trip of a lifetime. With no screw ups. And don't get us lost." No pressure.

I've worked in development for 20 years, and this European Tour Director Training Program is still right up there with the most intensive bodies of development I've undertaken – and it was my first! Despite the high intensity, it was also the most enjoyable. As I began to run these development sessions, I discovered two critical foundations regarding human development and peak performance.

1: The key to success is constant up-skilling

As a tour director, you'd have to face different cities and different logistics year on year. Sometimes entire countries would either cease to exist or be born again. You'd have to keep a calm head about you and your knowledge up to speed to remain credible and become a master at your craft. In all fields of human endeavour, the ability to keep up to date and think ahead is fundamental. If the Wright brothers were still alive today, what's the likelihood they'd still be producing single-person planes with a maximum speed of 48km/h?

Keep developing a range of skills: soft (time management, problem-solving, communication), hard (software, reading, math), intellectual (critical analysis, assimilation of new knowledge), and emotional (ability to manage anger, sadness, anxiety and joy). You'll be prepared for anything.

Be sure to choose development programs that align with your overall goals, regardless of whether you are an individual looking to improve or a leader driving programs. Then only choose programs that can be measured against objective metrics or results. Be it personal or professional, there's no reason to see adapting or development as novel or a waste of time if the results stack up.

2: Be adaptable

It's been a long time since I ran a European Tour Director Program. While some training requirements have probably changed, there's one thing that never will: a tour director must always know where they are going.

Firstly, because drivers must feel confident in finding their way around Europe. Secondly, because getting lost really annoys passengers.

Back in the early 1990s, GPS wasn't standard, so we'd show trainees how to adopt a simple, yet effective, method of getting around in the form of shorthand route notes. By swiftly and systematically documenting a directional arrow, a landmark and preceding it with a rudimentary running time check, you'd have an efficient handwritten GPPS: Global Pencilled Positioning System. A hard copy you could refer to anytime.

Route notes these days are far more efficient thanks to accessible and reasonably priced interactive mapping tools. Even localised maps for city walking tours are now in everyone's hands through a combination of Google Maps and smartphones.

While development tools have shifted from manual to digital, there are many other instances where subtle changes have an equally powerful impact on overall performance. You need to be able to adapt to these.

Having insight into your chosen profession falls into this category. In the touring world, having insight into a city prevents major debacles.

There's nothing worse than hyping up your passengers, then turning up to a major tourist attraction only to find it's been closed temporarily for renovations. Oops! In all industries, things change so rapidly that not reading or keeping abreast of knowledge and trends will leave you falling behind.

Most people realise the importance of adaption, yet often the concept is one that may happen reactively rather than pro-actively. Yes, development and adapting take time, but so does anything in life that is worth doing. Becoming too busy to learn and consciously challenge ourselves consciously is easy. Time invested in development, with equal consideration for other priorities, is essential.

Build time into your calendar, be it weekly, monthly or quarterly. Then commit, rather than sacrifice, the time for the growth and evolution of your mind. Having a strategy for your development is in itself a simple way to make sure you remain adaptable.

Keep in mind that there is a difference between knowing you should adapt, and actually doing so.

Awareness of the importance of adapting doesn't deliver measurable results. Any knowledge remaining merely as a theory, floating in the ether, scribbled on notepads, discussed in a brainstorm or loosely set as a goal are also a waste of time. Any fantastic ideas relating to adaption are simply shiny objects lit once for entertainment, then left to fizzle out. If you're going to adapt, you must commit to putting knowledge and tools into action, and continually challenge the status quo to place you outside of your comfort zone. Setting and having defined SMART goals (see Chapter 10) means you'll be able to not only roll with the punches, but stay ahead of them.

You also need to remember that technology isn't the answer to everything. Make no bones about it, the speed and variety of technology advancements mean tech has become a core focus of adaptation, and rightly so. The problem with adapting to technology is that its greatest strength can also become our greatest weakness. The more connected we are, the more disconnected we become. We are still human beings who experience our world through the senses (see Chapter Four) – the five obvious ones being sight, sound, smell, touch and taste, and even the more subtle ones such as the sense of balance, or that enigmatic sixth sense of intuition. We can't rely on technology to replace the natural energetic drive that human interaction thrives on. If you want to be truly adaptable, learn to log off and tune back into your old school, hard-wired operating systems.

It's also important to ask for help and input from others. While change and adaptability happen at an individual level, we are never truly alone. If we aren't open to collaboration with others, we run the risk of shutting off from the very things that could benefit us. Being open to feedback and asking for input is the ultimate form of adaption.

Ongoing development and adaptability are key landmarks on the road to success. Allowing time for them ensures that when we check in, update or do a complete reboot in any area of life, we'll be doing so with the best route notes to get us there.

Tarot: Tower

The image of a tower on the Tower card signifies ambitions built on false premises, while a lightning bolt represents a breakdown of existing forms to make rooms for new ones. Drawing this card serves as a reminder that it's possible to become too comfortable in the narrow confines of your life until something shocking comes along and destroys your picture of peace and harmony. We are reminded to consider how we will manage such a shake-up. In times of major upheaval, it's important to ask yourself where the turmoil lies, and how to create new beginnings. The Tower also signifies the inner and outer structures you have built - your walls and your defences. We must live under the impression that these walls could come down at any moment to reveal our inner world. Drawing this card means you need to break down those structures you have built and adapt to a more open and honest way of living. You must embrace the opportunity to accept change and be prepared to move forward into a more positive psychological state. Although the journey there may be tough, the personal freedom it will bring is worth it.

Illustration:

A beautiful pearl can only be formed when an irritant enters the shell of a oyster. Fluid continues to wrap itself around the deposit until the gleaming, perfect, lustrous sphere is formed. The pearl hints that adaptability, no matter the situation, leads to fruitful and valuable outcomes. The chameleon, another of nature's masters of metamorphosis, clutches the precious gem.

Three quick tips:

- Shake things up by changing your routine every now and again
- Train your mind to see change as an opportunity
- Use Edward de Bono's Six Thinking Hats to challenge your view on a particular task or situation

A dream is just a dream. A goal is a dream with a plan and a deadline.

- Harvey Mackay

Chapter Ten

Goals

"All men dream but not equally. Those who dream by night in the dusty recesses of their minds wake in the day to find that it was vanity, but the dreamers of the day are dangerous for they may act on their dreams with open eyes to make it possible." – T.E. Lawrence

Dream catchers - Dream legend

The origin of the dream catcher can be traced back to Ojibwe, one of the largest American Indian tribes. It was only in the 20th century that the use of dream catchers was made accessible outside the realms of American Indian tradition. The American Indians believed the night air was full of dreams – the good, the bad, and the downright ugly. By hanging a dream catcher above your sleeping head, you could purify your dreams. The nightmares were caught in the net, and the sweet ones driped down the feathers into your subconscious.

Each element of the traditional dream catcher serves a powerfully symbolic purpose. The round hoop represents the movement of the sun and the moon. It was believed that nightmares were born in the dark and destroyed in the light, so the hoop's web would catch the nightmares and detain them until the sun's rays could destroy them.

The sweet dreams were allowed to flow freely to the sleeping person to become fuel for creativity unencumbered by harmful subconscious imagery from nightmares. Traditional dream catchers were built from natural, degradable materials, like willows for the hoops, twine or vine for the woven web, and real feathers found on the ground. The idea was for a child's dream catcher to degrade over time so by the time they reach adulthood, their childish fears and desires had disintegrated and returned to the earth.

Dream Catchers – my personal approach

I've always loved the philosophy of dream catchers. Hand making them is a therapeutic, tactile creative outlet that is very different from the mental energy and focus it takes to build keynote and development program content. I was making dream catchers long before I realised my brand initials were slap bang in the middle.

So my adapted versions became dreaMCatchers. Each dreaMCatcher is built for a particular owner or theme through carefully chosen colours and charms, including precious and semi-precious stones. They can take anywhere from two to eight hours to build, depending on the size and complexity. While I've improved my methods over time, I'm no natural weaver. They can be tricky little suckers to make. Then again, the imperfections are what make them unique. And no one has complained so far!

I've crafted a dreaMCatcher with a web that featured fine dining cutlery, graceful feathers, and thick twirls of red, white and blue as a nod to the baroque style at request from my best mate and fine dining French chef, Manu Prudhomme.

I've built a massive Fitness First-inspired dreaMCatcher that took nine hours to create after sourcing all the required resources. The hoop and web was a bicycle wheel that was then decorated with 3kg of training-themed charms: skipping rope, free weights, mini boxing gloves, tiny runners, metal chains, weight clips and 13 metres of rope, in the color of Fitness First brand.

All have been made with care and freely gifted to people in my circle or as a giveaway to inspire motivation and action towards personal goals. Some have been exceptionally personal, channeling love and respect for the intended recipient. You can view the collection on my website.

I'm aware that making dream catchers could be considered as culturally disrespectful given I'm not from an American Indian tribe. However, My dreaMCatchers are always made as gifts and not for commercial gain.

While dreams – the kind you have when you're awake – are intrinsically linked to my line of work, I'm also fascinated by cultures where unconscious dreaming is intrinsically linked to their waking lives. Along with Indian American dream culture, I'm interested in the Indigenous Australian Dreamtime.

In my experience as a tour guide, Australians would visit Europe and lament the lack of history on their home turf. I went to great lengths to explain that while they might not have visible access to history, like the Colosseum in Rome, their country had a rich verbal history that dates back somewhere between 40,000-80,000 years. It's called the Dreamtime.

As far as the oral history of Dreamtime goes, the story of the rainbow serpent is far more interesting than the Roman viaduct water transportation. Legend has it that a massive rainbow serpent rose from beneath the ground, and as it wiggled and slivered, it forged gorges that became rivers and valleys, essentially giving life to the arid Australian landscape. And if it's visual history you want, look no further than the earliest known Indigenous rock paintings that precede the earliest known Roman rock paintings by many thousands of years.

The Dreamtime is an intrinsic part of Indigenous Australian history. It dictates beliefs, rules, and values within society. Dreamtime represents everything that has, is, and ever will be. It exists beyond time and space.

I'm also interested in the scientific study of dreams. Most dreams occur in the Rapid Eye Movement (REM) state of sleep where our brain activity is high and resembles consciousness without us being awake. The dreams that occur during REM are the ones we're most likely to remember.

There are plenty of hypothesis surrounding dreams, sleep, and premonitions, but with science and technology constantly evolving, we don't have any accuracy surrounding how or why we dream. We laugh at the science of 300 years ago, and in another 300 years, the people of the future will probably laugh at us.

We've probably all had dreams and epiphanies that no science model could explain – epiphanies that could make even the hardest pragmatist stop in their tracks. The only thing I know for sure is that dreams that are sparked in the subconscious can be powerful and have the ability to influence reality when we pay attention to them and consciously respond.

Certainly, dreams can come true if you have the grit and determination to pursue them.

The difference between a dream and a goal is the existence of a distinct plan and a deadline. What T.E Lawerence was getting at, was that dreams without direction are just a little too esoteric – they're a tad too flighty. Creating a map of actions that will lead you towards your goal is a significant step towards achieving the as-yet-unattainable, i.e. your dream. This is the dreaming you do with your eyes open.

Here are some tips to help you transform your dreams into reality:

1: Let your vision fuel the dream machine

Think of your actions as mechanisms in the Dream Machine, and think of your vision as the fuel that powers that machine. For the machine to run smoothly from A (your initial idea) to B (the end goal), all parts need to be in working order and they need to work together – this is where you need an action plan.

Let's use grocery shopping as an example. When you realise your cupboards are bare, you drive to the store with a purpose: to replenish your pantry. The dream (goal) here is a fully stocked pantry; the Dream Machine is your car; the fuel is your hunger.

2: Be flexible

Imagine your car breaks down on your way to the grocery store. If you're desperate enough, you'll find another way of getting there (taxi, bus, train, or a lift from a friend). But if you've got two slices of bread left in the freezer and a tin of tuna, then your desperation has diminished, and there's a good chance that having toast for dinner is easier than finding or paying for an alternative way to get to the supermarket. You'll settle for what you already have after being derailed by one obstacle.

If you're hungry enough, you'll find a way to adapt. You might come across something you never expected, like a restaurant on the corner that you would have missed if you didn't take an alternate route.

In his book, Seven Spiritual Laws of Success, Deepak Chopra talks about the principle of detachment. This is where, to achieve your goals, you stop trying to force things into happening. Yes, plan your map to success and aim for goals that align with your natural gifts and strengths, however, don't get so attached to every pit stop that you miss out on something even better along the way. Being detached means being flexible.

3: Be accountable

There are many goal-setting models designed to keep you on track. Here are some of the most common ones:

S.M.A.R.T

Specific – **M**easurable – **A**chievable – **R**ealistic – **T**imeframe

H.A.R.D

Heartfelt – **A**nimated – **R**equired – **D**ifficult

Q.U.E.S.T

Qualities – **U**nderstanding – **E**xpertise – **S**trategic Thinking – **T**ime

A D.R.E.A.M

A **D**aily **R**egime **E**nabling **A**ppropriate **M**omentum

Some other ideas:

- Write your goals in vivid detail and the present tense, as if they are happening now
- Record yourself talking about your goals and listen to the recording as you fall asleep

- Create a visual depiction of your goals, like a storyboard to remind you of where you want to be

It's important to find the method that works best for you and update it periodically to ensure you're still on track, especially if you need to reroute due to a setback.

In the series, *Redesign My Brain*, Todd Sampson conducts a brain makeover using cutting-edge brain training, tests and tools created by leading neuroscientists.

One episode sees him trying to improve his brain performance by holding his breath underwater while trying to escape from 25 feet of chain and five combination locks – something Houdini never even tried. To help him succeed, the Australian Institute of Sport included visualisation as a part of his training. The process of visualisation – the idea that mentally performing a task can be as beneficial as physically doing it – is a valid tool used by psychologists and professional athletes around the world.

During another challenge, Sampson has to throw darts with his non-preferred hand and aim to hit bull's eye. He's hooked up to a device that measures his muscle contraction and tracks his sight. On his first try, he scores an accuracy of 27%, eye tracking ability of 31% and arm muscle efficiency of 33%. He's then sent away for a month to practise, without throwing a single dart. For a mere five minutes a day, five days a week for four weeks, all he has to do is visualise throwing the dart and hitting the target. When it comes to the real thing, Sampson notices that not only did task seem easier, but the tangible improvement was huge: accuracy of 58%, eye tracking ability of 53%, and arm muscle efficiency of 52%. He almost doubled his scores across the board simply from imagination.

Tarot: Moon

The Moon represents intuition, dreams, and the unconscious. The Moon casts a dim light on the Earth as it reflects the sun, only vaguely illuminating our path through the darkness. The card often depicts a pool, representing the subconscious mind, and the creatures crawling out of the water represent the early stages of consciousness. The creatures also remind us of the disturbing images that our unconscious mind is capable of conjuring in nightmares. There is a path guarded by a dog and a wolf – representing the tame and wild aspects of our minds – that leads to mountains in the distance. This is the way to the unconscious. The idea of the Moon is to illuminate the darkness – to prevent deceptions and distortions of the truth and to ensure we don't accidentally stray from our path.

Illustration:

The dream catcher's charms suggest differing types of goals: performance, learning, and fulfillment. The idea of the handmade web, filtering out negativity and thoughts that serve to hold us back, is continued in the background in a shadow of intricate beauty and design.

Three quick tips:

- Visualise, write down, or record your goals and frequently remind yourself of them
- Make sure your goals are specific and achievable
- Share your goals with someone who you know will keep you in check

Productivity is never an accident, it is always the result of a commitment to excellence, intelligent planning and focussed effort.

- Paul J Meyer

Chapter Eleven
Productivity

The Power Hour

Urban legend has it that the original Power Hour was a drinking game where you'd down a shot of booze for every passing minute (not the most productive way to spend an hour, but you get the idea).

Back in 1876, Frank Dodds completed a more civilised Power Hour when he pedalled more than 25km around the Cambridge University grounds on a penny-farthing. Now, the distance pedalled in that time has more than doubled – some have travelled over 90km thanks to contemporary equipment.

Barista and co-owner of Atlas Espresso in Hobart, Suzanne Stagg set the Guinness World Record when she frothed up a staggering 289 cappuccinos in 60 minutes.

In collaboration with the E! Network, barber Julian Payne completed 72 buzz cuts in the lead up to the 2014 Oscars red carpet coverage.

The Queensland chapter of the Australian Institute of Management clocked in 475 participants for 21 speed network meetings – each participant had at least 20 meetings within the hour.

We can take the idea of the Power Hour into our everyday lives, even if we're not trying to break records.

One hour of absolute power where you do the maximum amount of (insert your chosen task here) in 60 minutes flat.

Three simple concepts can help you to focus your attention and energy towards achieving specific goals:

1: Be where you are

Stay focussed on the primary task at hand without distraction. Even the two seconds it takes to check Facebook can sidetrack you.

2: Apply best practice to each part of the task

Be consistent in your approach to each element. Give 100 per cent, 100 per cent of the time.

3: Apply a happy disposition and great mental attitude

It is near impossible to do good work when your heart and mind aren't in it. If you're in a foul mood, don't attempt major tasks – start with something smaller and work your way up if and as your mood gets better. It's a good idea to budget some bad mood time – an hour or two worked into your timeframe where you don't have to feel guilty about taking some time out. You'll be more productive for it.

Productivity

The days you feel most on track probably aren't the ones you spend lounging around watching back-to-back episodes of *Game of Thrones*. Days of absolute fulfilment and productivity are the ones when, as Margaret Thatcher would say, "you've had everything to do and you've done it."

Productivity often involves the juggling of many tasks. The mind multi-tasks in three ways:

- Conscious or unconscious habit requiring little to no thought, like changing gears while driving
- Toggling between brain functions, like reading a book while listening to music
- Focussing on priorities, like choosing one task and concentrating on that until it's done.

To be more productive, you need to learn to focus your attention. Here are 10 tips to help you master, or at least improve, your productivity:

1: Become a postage stamp

"The interesting thing about a postage stamp is the persistence with which it sticks to its job." - Napoleon Hill

Prioritising, and then sticking to your task is a sure-fire way of improving your productivity. When you complete one big task, the smaller ones are easier to tackle – you'll see that to-do list dwindling in no time!

Write down your six most pressing priorities and work through them in order. Don't allow yourself any distractions. If you're working with a larger group, at school or work, encourage the key leaders to do the same thing.

To determine which are your most pressing tasks, take a look at some levellers. These could be due dates, revenue creation, customer satisfaction, and long-term goals, to name just a few.

Once identified, become the postage stamp: stick to the task at hand until it's delivered.

2: Minimise distractions

The world is full of distractions vying for your attention, conspiring to take you out of The Zone.

Don't let them do so. Take a moment to list your major distractions. These could include other people, noise, the Internet, social media, coffee and cigarette breaks. Once you've identified your particular distractions, you'll be more aware of when they come up, so you'll be better able avoid them.

3: Take regular breaks

You don't need to avoid distractions entirely – if you schedule in time to indulge in your favourite vices, you'll be less likely to come up against them throughout the day. Taking intentional breaks makes it easier for you to stick to your task because you'll be regenerated and refreshed, and less likely to log back into Facebook just in case something has happened in the last five minutes.

4: Plan in advance

"Don't put off until tomorrow what you can do today." - Benjamin Franklin

Take the extra effort to complete a task before the end of the day. It's a good way to wrap things up because you'll be left with a feeling of success and won't have to start the next day trying to remember where you left off.

5: Eliminate unnecessary meetings

An unnecessary meeting is the biggest killer to productivity. Everyone's been to (at least!) one meeting that could have been addressed by email instead. Consider the following before you accept the next invite:

- Is there a clear agenda?
- How long will it last?
- Does the topic require a meeting? Or is it a simple announcement?
- How many people are going? Often, too many people can limit results

6: Stop reacting

Are you guilty of immediately stopping in your tracks when you see a notification flash up in the corner of your screen? Do you feel the need to check it and respond straight away?

There's no need to feel anxious about not responding to emails and messages straight away – everyone is just as time-poor as you and don't expect you to be able to answer to every ping within seconds. You, as well as everyone you communicate with, will be more productive if you set boundaries around time frames for email requests and replies.

Once you set your boundaries (E.g. having a list of people who need to be responded to immediately, like your boss, and a list of ad hoc emails that can wait), make sure you stick to them. Set aside an hour to work through your emails systematically and you might find that you are more productive throughout the day.

7: Delegate

If you consider yourself a Jack-of-all-trades, you may find yourself the master of none. No one is good at everything – as Einstein said, "Everybody is a genius. But if you judge a fish by its ability to climb a tree, it will live its whole life believing that it is stupid."

If you find yourself ill-equipped to handle a task on your own, it's wise to approach someone who is skilled in that arena. For example, if you're an accountant who thinks Microsoft Paint can be used to make your website, try to find a web developer who knows how to code instead. Asking for help, or delegating tasks, gives you the opportunity to work with masterminds and streamline your productivity. You'll also have more time to focus on what you enjoy, as well as are good at. (Hint: take note if these are two different things.)

8: Renewal

Physical renewal: eating, exercise and sleep

Social renewal: meaningful (rather than meaningless) connections and conversations

Spiritual renewal: meditation, creative arts or simple quiet time

Mental renewal: learning, reading or teaching

While all renewal in all of these areas is necessary, I want to focus here on mental renewal. Up-skilling and developing yourself in areas specific to your career and your goals will impact your productivity long-term.

As John F Kennedy said, "Leadership and learning are indispensable to each other."

9: Face the mirror

As you would have read in Chapter Six, the art of self-control is vital to productivity. Being able to face the mirror allows for honest self-assessment. Take a good hard look at your actions and ask yourself, what is it that motivates and inspires you? What is it that gets you in the zone? Find what it is that keeps you focussed on a task and stick to it until completion.

10: Learn to truly value your time

The more productive you become, the more you will start to appreciate your time. You'll start to realise who and what is worth spending your precious time on, as well as how much time you are willing to invest in individual projects.

Tarot: The Emperor

The Emperor represents power and authority, and his long grey beard is a symbol of his experience. He's acquired years of wisdom. He's learned from his mistakes and understands that all actions – positive or negative – have consequences. His throne is decorated with ram's heads that represent intellectual heights, determination, effort, initiative and leadership. The Emperor is also able to create order out of chaos by mapping out his thoughts and making solid plans as to what needs to be done to solve a problem or achieve a goal. He respects rules, boundaries and routine.

Illustration:

In our updated Productivity card, the hourglass represents time – how you value it and use it. Time is your most precious commodity given that once you spend it you will never get it back. The staircase leading to the top of the hourglass signifies that success can be achieved one step at a time. You must keep moving forward towards your goals. The heavy cogs turning in the background represent noise and distraction, yet our focus remains on the hourglass and on our productivity.

Three quick tips:

- Focus on less in order to get more done
- Stick to your priority tasks and goals
- Minimise your distractions

Consistent action creates consistent results.
- Christine Kane

Chapter Twelve
Consistency

Lessons from Winston Churchill

Winston Churchill was the epitome of persistence and consistency.

Before World War I broke out, he served as First Lord of the Admiralty (essentially President of the Board of Admiralty in the British Navy) until the disastrous Gallipoli campaigns forced him out of government and into the political wilderness. He resurfaced to become Prime Minister in 1940 and lead Britain through the dark days of World War II. He served as PM again from 1951-1955.

His first speech as Prime Minister on 10 May 1940 hinted at the hardships the county would have to endure: "You ask what is our aim? I can answer in one word: victory; victory at all costs, victory in spite of all terror, victory, however long and hard the road may be; for without victory, there is no survival."

Within days of making the speech, Churchill was faced with the German invasion of the Netherlands, Belgium, Luxembourg and France, leaving Britain to stand alone. Churchill took swift action, forming an alliance with the United States and the Soviet Union. His tenacious attitude and determination to keep his aim of victory alive is seen in his address to the House of Commons on 4 June 1940:

> *We shall go on to the end. We shall fight in France, we shall fight on the seas and oceans, we shall fight with growing confidence and growing strength in the air. We shall defend our island, whatever the cost may be. We shall fight on the beaches, we shall fight on the landing grounds, we shall fight in the fields and in the streets, we shall fight in the hills; we shall never surrender.*

But with Europe under German occupation before the US' entry into the war, the odds were stacked against Churchill and victory seemed out of reach. Yet he remained steadfast.

> *If we can stand up to [Hitler], all Europe may be freed and the life of the world may move forward into broad, sunlit uplands. But if we fail, then the whole world, including the United States, including all that that we have known and cared for, will sink into the abyss of a new dark age made more sinister, and perhaps more protracted, by the lights of perverted science. Let us, therefore, brace ourselves to our duties, and so bear ourselves, that if the British Empire and its Commonwealth last for a thousand years, men will still say, this was their finest hour.*

The Battle of Britain was an aerial battle of biblical proportions: a battle between good and evil that took place in the heavens, leaving vast destruction on Earth. The Battle lasted 112 days, from 10 July to 31 October 1940. Approximately 1,000 British and 2,000 German aircraft were brought down, killing 540 and 2,500 pilots respectively. It is estimated that over 40,000 civilians lost their lives in waves of nightly German attacks designed to break the British spirit and put an end to their war efforts.

Churchill once again rallied the country's spirit in one of his most memorable speeches:

> *The gratitude of every home in our island, in our Empire, and indeed throughout the world, except in the abodes of the guilty, goes out to the British airmen who, undaunted by odds, unwearied in their constant challenge and mortal danger, are turning the tide of the World War by their prowess and by their devotion. Never in the field of human conflict was so much owed by so many to so few.*

The British did indeed endure, and ultimately claimed the victory that Churchill so adamantly strove for (along with the US, USSR and France, of course). You don't need to be at war to understand how Churchill's stance on perseverance is relevant in all areas of life. Here are few more nuggets of wisdom from the man himself:

- "Continuous effort – not strength or intelligence – is the key to unlocking our potential."
- "Success is not final, failure is not fatal: it is the courage to continue that counts."
- "If you're going through hell, keep going."

Consistency and perseverance should accompany one another, hand in hand.

Five tips for success:

1: Where words like confidence, collaboration, courage, class, and candour often appear on the ingredient list for success, but one important word is often left out: consistency. Without consistency, all other elements of success begin to crumble, like a poorly made cake.

2: As in all areas of life, like kick-starting a new fitness regime or learning a new skill, it's consistency that determines how far you get. You can't do three sit-ups once a month and expect to see abs. You must be consistent in your consistency, too: don't be consistent with one short-term goal but intermittent with another. You must be consistent in your behaviour, self-control and attitude.

3: By consistently pursuing personal growth, you can increase your armoury of tools and skills. Contrary to the words of Oscar Wilde, who labelled consistency as "the last refuge of the unimaginative," your deftness for ongoing development ensures you remain a solid pillar of stability in the eyes of others without becoming mundanely predictable.

4: By continually evolving and tapping into your personal potential, you can lead with and enhance your strengths, while managing your weaknesses – allowing you to thrive and flourish. Consistency is the drip that creates ripple effects far into your future from where you stand right now.

5: People who live extraordinary lives have no secret weapons or tricks up their sleeves; they are very ordinary people. An extraordinary life is simply a life that is made up of hundreds of thousands of ordinary moments that are fused together with consistency. Consistency is an ongoing commitment to the self.

Five quick tips for creating consistency:

1: Minimise or eliminate self-sabotaging negative thinking

Other people don't make or break our habits. The start- and end-point for success often come when we fall on our sword. So, learn to smite down the negative nay-sayer inside your head. Flip the switch from problem to solution thinking (see Chapter Six), master your mind and "keep your hand firmly upon the helm of our thoughts" as author James Allen would say.

2: Appreciate the value of time

There is only now. The future is a theoretical concept until it happens, the past has been and gone. It's your actions now which create momentum towards success in all areas of life.

Procrastinate slightly less. Be a little more decisive. Living for the now with firm commitment will ultimately move you towards your personal fulfilment and success.

3: Make definite goals and action plans

Setting goals and making maps that will lead you to your goals will help you to sustain your drive, especially when you've identified your intrinsic motivator (see Chapter 10).

Start with your 'why'. Establish direction. Stick to the map, deviating if you must, but always keep the end destination in mind.

4: Challenges and emotional reactions are all fleeting

There's an expression I've always loved: "It's not what happens that's important. It's how you choose to respond."

Everything either passes or progresses. Learn to manage your emotional response to all situations outside of your direct control. (See Chapter Two.)

5: Make sure your words and actions are aligned

When someone says one thing and proceeds to do something entirely different, I've learned to pay attention to their actions. For, at that moment in time – in the now – their present modus operandi is the truest indicator of what they are making a stand for. In fact, in another article, The Elephant in the Room (see Chapter 20), I go as far to say "any words you may yell or scream are lost to the cacophony of noise your actions make".

Make sure what you say and what you do are completely aligned, so you can demonstrate integrity to others.

Also, when your thoughts and feelings are aligned with your words and actions, you have achieved consistent integrity within yourself.

Tarot: The Magician

The Magician is associated with skill, logic and intellect – all crucial elements for success. The Magician holds a staff in his left hand – one end pointing to the sky, the other towards the Earth – to take the power of the universe, channel it through his body, and direct it into the physical plane to get results. On the table sits all four suits of the Tarot to symbolise the appropriate use of mind, heart, body and soul in the process of manifestation. The Magician is a reminder to stay focussed on your goals, realise your potential and your conscious awareness towards continued action.

Illustration:

The organic rattan target signifies the idea of gaining rhythm through repetitive attempts, finding your stride, and ultimately succeeding. The target hangs on a locked door that is adorned with a repetitive pattern. From the handle hangs the Key of Consistency. We can see prior efforts of the marksman through the wear and tear of the target. Never the less, the bullseye, now loaded with strikes, highlights his consistent effort and practise. He got there in the end.

Three quick tips:

- Make sure your words and actions are aligned
- On the days you are feeling challenged and unmotivated, do it anyway
- Keep your eyes on your commitments stay accountable by checking in with yourself along the way

Creativity is a wild mind and a disciplined eye.

- Dorothy Parker

Chapter Thirteen
Creativity

The Original Baroque and Roller

There are many reasons I love visiting Vienna: the schnapps, the schnitzels, the Sachertorte. But the greatest reason for visiting Vienna is to see the classical concerts. These concerts play out in a handful of majestic palaces, and all pay tribute to the prolific Wolfgang Amadeus Mozart.

You probably wouldn't think it now, but Mozart was a disruptive rock star in his day. Born on 27 January 1756, his early years make Michael Jackson look like a late starter. At the age of four, he could play a piece of music within half an hour of hearing it for the first time. At five, he began writing minuets. He was touring and making public appearances, and even played for the Empress Maria Theresa at the tender age of six – a time when most of us are realising that paste glue isn't food.

He was eventually to move from his native Salzburg to Vienna, and it was here that he played concerts and received many accolades. Like many modern day celebrities, he was a passionate, stubborn, and had tremendous talent.

Mozart was quite simply a creative master at his craft. Imagine Elvis Presley's sexually provocative style and presence when he first arrived on the scene, and this would not be unlike the radical shockwaves that Mozart created. He challenged and disrupted the establishment, turning over 600 pieces of work before he died at the age of 35.

Palais Liechtenstein, 8 pm, August 23rd, 2001

Tonight we're going to experience a little of Mozart's genius with an orchestra at the ornate City Garden at Palais Liechtenstein.

Evenings such as this have a certain level of expectation as far as etiquette is concerned. It's pretty easy to pick up on the prompts and the silence pauses – when a mild applause is appropriate or if silence is better.

We enter a grand hall packed with pillars, portraits and paintings. Several sparkling chandeliers hang from the ceiling. The orchestra, in colourful pantaloons, bright tails and cream wigs, emerges from a door at the back.

A hush comes over the room as the conductor exaggerates his opening movement. His baton threatens the orchestra like a bolt of lightning. As he drops his hands in passionate fury, the strings fire up, the faces of the musicians contort with concentration. Even the triangle player (see Chapter 19) is captivating. The audience is lapping it all up. They love every moment.

9pm

We're about to be entertained by the rather upbeat *Die Entführung Aus Dem Serail* when things take a rather creative turn.

A guy from our group (let's call him Shane) decides to disrupt the entire performance silently.

He stands up, clutching an air guitar and begins to sync to the music – this is surely against etiquette. The ushers look anxiously at each other, trying to determine whether to stop him, or whether stopping him would be even more disruptive. They decide to leave him alone. The orchestra keeps playing. The audience's attention gradually moves from the on-stage performance to focus on the one happening in the seats.

Towards the end of the song, the two ushers have had enough of Shane's AC/DC style headbanging and tiptoe towards him to get him to stop.

Minutes later

When I asked Shane why he did what he did, he said that a little known town called Oulu, in Finland, was hosting the World Air Guitar Championship right now and if he weren't in Vienna, he'd be shredding silently right there. He even planned to compete the following year when the competition would be hosted in Australia.

It dawned on me then that, while we all thought Shane was insane, Mozart probably would have appreciated the eccentric, disruptive input. Especially given that Mozart was the original Baroque and Roller!

We can all take a leaf out of Mozart and Shane's books to creatively disrupt the status quo. It's easy to get caught up in the everyday, mindlessly completing the tasks on your roadmap that will lead you to your goal, but it's important to shake things up occasionally to keep things interesting and make sure you're still having fun.

Tarot: Empress

The Empress is ruled by Venus, the planet of love, creativity, fertility, art, beauty and grace. She represents a profound connection with the feminine - beauty, sensuality, and creative expression. She calls on us to connect with our creative energy so we can discover new ways of expressing ourselves and enter into a different frame of mind. The Empress also represents birth - the birth of a new idea, a new product, or a new way of being, and encourages us to bring forth all those ideas we have brewing inside us.

Illustration:

The Goddess-like figure, merging with the boundless potential that exists within the universe, is a reflection of the creative Empress. She gracefully commands forth all forms of creative expression and ingenuity into reality. Her free-flowing locks demonstrative of the notion that there is no right or wrong when it comes to creativity. You just need to let it flow.

Three quick, disruptive tips:

- Break the routine – wear your watch on the other hand, try a different coffee in the morning, take a different route or mode of transportation. The size of the disruptive experience doesn't matter, as long as they take you out of autopilot and give you a chance to experience the world.
- Encourage new and inspirational thoughts with word puzzles and games
- Try to meditate to clear the way for some creative thoughts

You have to do it by yourself, and you can't do it alone.

- Martin Rutte

Chapter Fourteen
Collaboration

Paris: from Podunk to prosperity

The city of light. The city of love. That's the paradigm that Paris has become.

Mind you; the city didn't start out this grand. When the area was originally settled back in 52BC, it wasn't so much a municipal as a Podunk – an island township known as Lutetia. A name you may recall if *Asterix the Gaul* adventures were a childhood reference point for anything historical.

The Seine River, now crossed and connected by 37 bridges, has been at the heart of the city from the very beginning, providing a bloodline for supply, shelter and sanctuary. Crossing one of the many bridges will take you to the founding island, the Île de la Cité upon which the mind-boggling, nearly-200-year long building project, known as Notre Dame sits. While Pope Alexander III laid the first stone in 1163, it was eventually completed in 1345, which is something to consider the next time you're frustrated by modern day delays.

Every monument has a fairytale-like name. Legends seep from every stone. Centuries of opulent dynasties, royal families and revolutionaries have left an indelible mark. And when it comes to the transformation of Paris from Podunk to prosperity, there were a few key players.

Napoléon Bonaparte, for one, breathed sweeping grandeur into the city, while Baron Haussmann implemented visionary town planning that streamlined efficiency and helped the city to become the epitome of elegance.

As time went on, the city inspired artworks from The Impressionists, like Manet and Monet, and their pieces now trade for millions at auction.

Through magnificent works of modernisation – including unique buildings like the inside-out Pompidou centre; the shimmering, bicentenary glass giant that is La Defense; I.M Pei's much-debated pyramid entrance to the Louvre – Paris has cemented itself as a city of stature and class.

Even McDonalds pays homage to the city's aesthetic. The franchise store perched on the Champs-Élysées (the most splendid thoroughfare known affectionately as 'the avenue of rubies and diamonds') has been adorned with subtle white arches instead of the brand's iconic golden ones.

I was fortunate enough to live in Paris for seven months, and made dozens of trips to the city while living elsewhere. I've come to recognise that even with its impressive illuminations, rich history, and overwhelming variety of museums, monuments and sights, Paris remains, at its heart and core, a city like every other. The French capital functions through an infrastructure hewn from stone, steel, blood, sweat, tales, tears and its people.

So, who is it that brought Paris from Podunk to prosperity? It was the believers: saints like St Genevieve and St Denis, who generated loyalty from others to form the basis of a faithful following.

It was the leaders: the kings like King Henry II, queens like Marie Antoinette, and decision-makers like Napoléon Bonapart who, for better or worse, commanded order and implemented systems of functionality.

It was the innovators: people like Baron Haussmann who had the foresight to widen boulevards and make way for the future.

It was the artists: Impressionists like Manet and Monet, Surrealists like Dali, the Cubists like Picasso, who took locals beyond logical thinking and into previously unimagined realms of the imagination.

It was the everyday people: the builders of the Notre Dame, who delivered results that stand the test of time.

Today it is the residents whose diligence and pride keeps the essential services running.

It is also the external advocates: The influential people who invest generously in helping drive the elevation of Paris to a prosperous, dizzying, five-star city.

In short, it was people. Paris' transition from Podunk to prosperity all comes down to the people and the collaboration of those people. The destiny of a city, like that of any business, is intrinsically tied to the devotion of your people. Investing, educating, nourishing, nurturing, challenging, supporting their talent will take your enterprise to dizzying new heights (like that of the Eiffel Tower).

Collaboration is a beacon of light. Collaboration enables possibilities that radiate love.

Tarot: The Hierophant

The Hierophant is also known as The High Priest. He represents a particular person, be it an advisor, a teacher or a guru, who should be trusted. He symbolises entry into all types of institutions where there is a shared group identity, like a school, team, company or society. The Hierophant represents institutions and their values; he shows us that sometimes we need to abide by established social structures and traditions. The focus here is on sharing and gaining knowledge through an institution or collaboration.

Illustration:

Collaboration is evident in the animal kingdom. Fish school with similar fish for defence and foraging. The same concept applies to like-minded individuals who work in collaboration; gracefully moving together to find and embrace harmonious, safe, productive flow.

Three quick tips:

- Participate in a mastermind group to transform ideas into something greater
- Be aware of individual communication styles, strengths and weaknesses
- Be willing to be vulnerable and open in your collaborations

Good timber does not grow with ease. The stronger wind, the stronger trees.

- Douglas Malloch

Chapter Fifteen
Challenge

The lady in the wheelchair and her mohair bear

Margarete Steiff, the founder of the Steiff toy company, was born in Giengen, Germany, on 24 July, 1847. After contracting polio as an infant, she was confined to a wheelchair for most of her life due to her legs being paralysed. She also suffered from extreme pain in her arm.

Despite her health issues, she harboured a desire to live a healthy life, so her siblings and neighbourhood friends would take her to school in a handcart, and then carry her into the classrooms. It was here Margarete decided, against her parents' wishes, to learn to sew.

In 1862, her loving sisters, Marie and Pauline, opened a dressmaker's shop where Margarete began working part time, and in 1877 she officially went into business on her own.

A few years later, Margarete stumbled upon patterns for small elephant cushions. It sparked her to start making elephant toys for kids, which soon became a best-selling product. By 1892, the range of fluffy toys included animals from every far-flung corner of the planet, and the company's motto became: "Only the best is good enough for your children."

In 1897, Maragarete's favourite nephew, Richard, joined her and they collaborated on fresh ideas, which resulted in the creation of one of the most famous children's toys on the planet: the teddy bear.

In 1903 they took the world by storm with the release of item 55 PB: a plush bear manufactured with mohair fur. The bear featured moveable arms and legs and was a huge success. By 1907, the company was producing 1.2 million toys, and the bears accounted for one million of them. They were called Teddy when they first hit the US market, as an homage to Theodore 'Teddy' Roosevelt. Legend has it that Roosevelt, an avid big game hunter, earned the nickname when he refused to shoot a bear that was tethered to a tree. Given the volumes of animals that fell to the crack of his rifle I don't think one could extend this act to his concerns for animal welfare, but somehow the nickname became synonymous with Margarete's creations.

The recognisable Steiff trademark was introduced in 1904. Steiff Bears were known for their high quality, and the branding was designed to help people avoid cheap imitations being replicated en masse.

They also save avid toy collectors from spending up big on a faux Steiff, and they really do spend big.

- The 1904 Teddy Girl exchanged hands for £110,000 in 1994.
- The 1908 blue Elliot bear sold for £49,500 in 1993.
- The 1912 Othello bear, one of six hundred produced to mourn the loss of RMS Titanic, sold for £91,750 in 2000.
- The 1926 Happy Bear fetched £55,000 in 1989.

Partnering with Louis Vuitton in 2000, around 90 years after Margarete's death, the company produced one of the most expensive teddy bears in the world. Adorned with a designer coat and hat, the bear was auctioned off, raising £130,190 for charity.

Margarete Steiff is a prime example of someone who had to challenge their capabilities. By setting herself a challenge (then learning skills required to achieve that challenge), she built a business and reputation synonymous with children's toys that still stands today.

Finding your flow

Mihaly Csikszentmihalyi, a professor of psychology, management, sociology and anthropology, dives into realms of happiness and creativity. Csikszentmihalyi is best known as the architect of the notion of personal flow, which is essentially a focussed mental state in which a person is performing an activity. The individual is so fully immersed in the process that it becomes fulfilling even to the point where one can lose conscious track or awareness of time. In sport, it's akin to being in the zone.

Take an Olympic sprinter, for example. While the sprint lasts around 10 seconds, it probably feels far longer, as if life is in slow motion. Someone taking part in a daylong activity, on the other hand, will probably feel like time has flown.

Csikszentmihalyi's Flow Theory uses a simple X-Y axis where vertical X-axis = Challenge and horizontal Y-axis = Skills. It highlights the importance of setting an appropriate challenge correlating an appropriate challenge that corresponds to your level of skill.

If the challenge is high and the skill set low, the challenge may create nervousness, frustration and resistance. Having to do this challenge once in a while or over a short period may not be detrimental, but doing it continuously without any improvement in skill is likely to cause anxiety. You can't get in the zone when you're anxious.

Conversely, if the challenge is low and the skill set is high, you might become bored or complacent. If you continue in this manner, you could become apathetic, which is hardly conducive to being in the zone.

The balance of finding your flow and being in The Zone then isn't static, given that skill sets and challenges are always changing because you're always learning. Every time you focus on a new task, your idea of what constitutes a challenge decreases.

An example from my field of work is presentation skills. Some people are scared to death of public presentations. To others, it's not such a big deal. Some people are bored to death analysing numbers, while others would thrive on the mathematic appeal of the task in hand. When setting ourselves a challenge it's important to consider a couple of the main aspects:

- What is it that excites or genuinely interests you?
- What are your strengths and weaknesses?
- What skills will you leverage or learn in pursuit of the task?

When pushing yourself beyond your comfort zone, do so with mindfulness, confidence and resilience.

Strive confidently towards challenges that you're willing to weather trials and tribulations for; challenges that take you out of your comfort zone. Challenges you believe are accomplishable without causing stress, anxiety, boredom or complacency.

Tarot: Hermit

The Hermit card shows a man standing on top of a mountain with a lantern in his hand. He is at his spiritual peak and is preparing to share his knowledge and light the way for others. While this is the pinnacle of one area of his life, he will continue on his path to the goal of ultimate awareness. Associated with the subconscious, The Hermit uses his isolation to increase his knowledge of the self. Drawing this card symbolises a period of reflection before making any decisions or facing any challenges.

Illustration:

A ship navigates a path through difficult and challenging waters. At first glance, the course appears to be a wild and treacherous ride, yet it's a route that's been consciously mapped by a commanding master. The captain steering the helm of thought knows that by leveraging and stretching all the skills at hand, the route set out will be surmountable. In the distance lies the arrival point of achievement basked in light and calm.

Three quick tips:

- Be aware of your strengths and weaknesses, and set yourself challenges that align with them and your goals
- Create a bucket list and then tick something off
- Do something you've been putting off for ages

Life has many ways of testing a person's will, either by having nothing happen at all or by having everything happen all at once.

- Paulo Coelho

Chapter Sixteen
Strength

Mining and polishing human diamonds

From their first recorded use in India around 6,000 years ago, through to current day, diamonds have been appraised as a valuable commodity in monetary and spiritual terms, from ancient talisman to a woman's best friend. Mind you, the dollar value given to diamonds is partially an illusion, given that amongst the Earth's gems, they are the most common. They're often priced well beyond other stones.

Diamonds are formed in the Earth's mantle and make their way to the surface by catching a wave of a deep-source volcanic eruption. During their journey to the top, they develop exceptional qualities that we can try to replicate in our human lives.

A diamond forms when carbon is placed under intense pressure. Considering the second most common element that exists in the human body is carbon, there's no reason why we can't hold up under pressure and come out the other side shiny and worth millions, right?

Maybe that's where the concept of referring to someone as a 'gem' originated. What's more, just like the diamonds, we also come in all sorts of unusual shapes, colours, sizes and multi-dimensional facets.

In leading dozens of tours across Europe – including side trips to points of interest such as Amsterdam's carbon rhombus merchants – I discovered the 5C model assessing the value of diamonds:

Cut – Colour – Clarity – Carat – Certification

If you were to adopt the qualities of a diamond in your attitude, values and actions in your everyday living, your character would reign supreme:

- Diamonds are the hardest known and most resilient natural material on the planet. You too can choose to become resilient. The fundamental principle of personal resilience dates as far back as 55AD to the Greek philosopher Epictetus, to who the notion: "It's not what happens to you, but how you react to it that matters," is credited. (See Chapter Two.)
- Diamonds can survive extreme pressures as well as physical, chemical or radioactive forces that would destroy other materials. Do not let external factors destroy you.
- *"'Pressure' is often a word misused in our vocabulary. When you start thinking of pressure, it's because you've started to think of failure."* - Coach Tommy Lasorda.
- Diamonds can act as either an insulator or conductor, allowing electricity and energy to be passed or blocked. Learn to insulate and magnify your energy to remain focused on the good that you desire. Block the naysayers and eliminate the negatives that hold you back. (See Chapter Seven.)
- Pure diamond is the most transparent material known, with the ability to reflect UV or infrared light spectrums and all frequencies in between. Be transparent in your actions, and concentrate on picking up the subtle frequencies of others.
- *"A lack of transparency results in distrust and a deep sense of insecurity."* - The Dalai Lama
- Visible imperfections and tiny cracks impact upon a diamond's clarity. These are akin to the life lessons that impact our beliefs or behaviours. People aren't broken; people acquire life experiences. Imperfection is, well, perfect.

- *"Imperfection is beauty, madness is genius, and it's better to be absolutely ridiculous than absolutely boring."* - Marilyn Monroe

Consider all the qualities of diamonds and imagine how you can adapt them to your life and career. Take into account the 5C model for humans to ensure you get the best cut and polish:

Confidence – Challenge – Creativity – Coaching - Culture

Confidence:

Confidence addresses both inner confidence and finding belief in products, services or causes to which you are aligned. (See Chapter One.)

Challenge:

Don't become complacent. Consider your goal from all angles to find new challenges that will keep you interested. (See Chapter 15)

Creativity:

Use your imagination. Shake up your routine. Pick up a hobby. (See Chapter 13.)

Coaching:

Continually adapt and up-skill to leverage your strengths and manage your weaknesses. Change is inevitable, but personal growth is always your decision.

Culture:

Surround yourself with people who support you. Create a culture with shared visions, values, beliefs, and habits.

Tarot: Strength

The traditional Strength card features elements that also appear on other cards, like the Magician's infinity symbol, the Fool's white robe, the Lovers' phallic mountains. The woman in the card demonstrates strength by taming a wild lion - you can see her patting the beast and smiling peacefully. She has overcome her fear of the lion through a quiet strength that can only come from within. The Strength card is more reflective of mental strength than physical strength and to draw it in a reading means that you need to know that you can endure life's obstacles and you have great stamina and persistence.

Illustration:

The tiger has long seen a symbol of overall power and strength. They base their decisions on sharp sight and heightened senses. The tiger fears nothing. Our white tiger's blue eyes also suit the blue hues of the chakra evolution in the deck. The regal monarch, king or queen of its territory, sits patiently alert guarding the parameters of its fort. A single gem of shining brilliance, the strongest substance known to man, stands out from a subtle diamond pattern and reiterates the facets of personal boundaries and strength.

Three quick tips:

- Increase your levels of empathy
- Back yourself once you've made decisions
- Pick your battles: know when to make a stand and when to walk away

Acceptance and tolerance and forgiveness, those are lifealtering lessons.

- Jessica Lange

Chapter Seventeen

Acceptance

Wonder Mum

I hope most people consider their mother a superhero.

In my case, it's closer to the truth than you can imagine.

My mum, Linda Bowler, married my father and became Linda Carter. While she spells Linda with an 'i' instead of a 'y', she still shared the name with the actress who played Wonder Woman, Lynda Carter.

My mum has since remarried and is now Linda Kaiser, but to me, she is still synonymous with Wonder Woman, even if the name has changed. So as a tribute to all superhero mums around the globe, here are eight things we can learn from our Wonder Mums.

1: Pain comes before the joy

My mother had three sons by the age of 21. As a male, I cannot imagine the pain and discomfort of pregnancy and birth, but my mother has always said it was always overridden by the joy of motherhood.

Apparently, I was an easy birth compared to my older brothers. An easy birth here is relative. Every mother has gone through some extent of hell so that we may be a part of this world. Mothers are bulletproof when it comes to enduring pain to bring joy.

The first lesson we can learn from our Wonder Mums is that we too may have to go through periods of pain to reach the joy. Embrace and endure. It will all be worth it.

2: Acceptance and forgiveness are a base operating system

My brothers and I drove my poor mum mental at times (especially my middle brother. (Never me, of course)).

But she always had a way of accepting and forgiving us for all our shortcomings. She still does, even though we're all adults now. The art of acceptance and forgiveness seems to be a stronger natural gift in mothers than many other human people.

If the ability to accept and forgive, the way other mothers do, were inherent human qualities, the world would surely be a better place.

If only we could find a way to harness, bottle and dispense acceptance and forgiveness as medicine – a modern day prescription for humanity.

3: Retirement isn't an option

Mothers don't get to retire. Motherhood is for life.

My mum was still sending me parcels with jocks and socks well into my 30s – I didn't have the heart to tell her I'd been buying my own in the correct size for years. Not only do mothers not get to retire, but the reward and recognition also leaves much to be desired.

Laundry, cooking, cleaning, nursing, problem solving and entertaining for years – to name but a few jobs – without pay.

Mums never get promoted. There's no career progression. They're literally in it for love.

That's a beautiful lesson I've had from my mum right there. In the same way that motherhood itself is a lifetime reward, make sure you're doing something you love to do. Don't worry about the surface, social success or recognition, which may or may not come as a result.

By doing things you love, you're more likely assured a full, rewarding life.

4: Even superheroes cuss

Mum would spit out her favourite cuss word in sheer frustration at times, which is hardly surprising when you have three young boys. As young kids, we would fight over toys and form bands with empty boxes for drums while yelling and swearing instead of singing. As we got older, we would play soccer in the hallway as if it were a full-sized football pitch. And then once we turned 18 we would come home after curfew and attempt to make a pizza, only to pass out in the process and fill the house with smoke from the oven.

I'm amazed the cussing was mostly limited to "Stop fart-arsing around!"

If you struggle with your time management or productivity, I'd highly encourage you to learn this Wonder Mum cuss. Write it down, laminate it, put it on your desk, lap it up, commit it to memory, say it to yourself aloud and hold yourself accountable. There are times in life where you just have to stop fart-arsing around and get meaningful s**t done instead.

5: The route you take is irrelevant; just get there safely

Wonder mum is the life of any party, yet she's completely hopeless when it comes to getting to the party in the first place.

Reading maps has never been my mum's high point. She knows front and back, and left and right – well, 90 percent of the time anyway – provided she hasn't topped off a couple of glasses of sauvignon blanc with brandy. "Going round in circles" in my Wonder Mum's case is a reality rather than a figure of speech.

Her old school, printed maps turn into tea coasters; Tom-Toms are confusing – which way are you facing? The little arrow keeps moving!

It takes more effort to try to translate the robotic GPS voice than it does just to drive in the right direction.

My mum never learnt to drive, so she doesn't care so much about the route, she just enjoys the journey. As long as you get to where you want to be, who cares how you got there? As long as you arrive safely.

It's easy to get fixated on your route, but it's equally important to be flexible. There are many different ways to reach a destination.

6: You have a voice, and you should use it

As a superheroine with public life as a librarian, mum lives by the philosophy that the pen is mightier than the sword. The 'pen' in any given situation could be beautifully written prose, or even a completely cutting spoken word.

I've seen train station masters, check-in counter clerks, naval officers, store managers and even random strangers put in their place after receiving a finger pointing or tongue lashing from Wonder Mum.

Lesson number six is that to get what you want, you need to learn to speak up. It's important to make a stand and be heard.

7: Take calculated risks

I asked my mum to share her life's philosophy. She said: "Take calculated risks. Recognise that whatever decision you make is the right one, and if it turns out pear-shaped, you can always make another choice."

Given she moved from Scotland to New Zealand at the age of 50, I see how she lives by this motto frequently. She accepts, adapts and changes. She takes risks, and if they don't work out, well it's just another story for the memoir. Those who take risks lead the most exciting lives. After all, no one's going to read a biography of The Man Who Sat Still And Did Nothing.

8: You can't always wave your magic wand

Mothers have a tendency to want to solve other people's problems; to wave a magic wand for the people about whom they care. Unfortunately, the concept of a magic wand is reserved for fairy tales, Hollywood blockbusters, and fantasy books (the kind you'd find on my mum's library shelves).

So, lesson number eight: when you're desperate for a magic wand, remember Wonder Mum's first lesson – accept the situation as it is, because the pain comes before joy.

While the connection between Wonder Woman and mothers may be clear, you might be wondering how it all connects to this chapter's theme of acceptance.

Wonder Woman's creator, William Moulton Marston, was a lawyer, inventor and psychologist. He believed that cartoons and visual storytelling were viable avenues for education.

Marston is credited with inventing systolic blood pressure testing – an integral part of the polygraph, or lie detector, tests. His fascination with discovering the truth may even have been the inspiration for his heroine's major weapon of choice: anyone caught in the whipping grasp of Wonder Woman's 'Lasso of Truth' was forced to give up the gospel.

Marston also published a paper in 1928 entitled *Emotions of Normal People*, in which he laid out theories and concepts that became the basis of DISC theory. DISC is a behaviour assessment tool based on four different behavioural traits. Originally those were dominance, inducement, submission, and compliance, but they have been changed to dominance, influence, steadiness, compliance.. It's perhaps one of the better-known behavioural science and profiling tools available on the market and one I am accredited in.

Marston's original paper proposed that behaviour was, in part, influenced by whether the person perceived of their environment as favourable or not. There have been suggestions that his work was based on lessons from his wife, Elizabeth who he noted, "when she got mad or excited, her blood pressure seemed to climb."

Marston saw women as being full of strength and power, while inherently more honest than men. So, throwing this all together, he moulded a superheroine of significant qualities who "would triumph not with fists or firepower, but with love."

Through the creation of Wonder Woman, he leveraged the vehicle of visual storytelling. He noted that "Comics speak, without qualm or sophistication, to the innermost ears of the wishful self. The response is like that of a thirsty traveller who suddenly finds water in the desert – he drinks to satiation." His style of storytelling certainly made an impact, and in fact, in 2006 he was inducted into the Comic Book Hall of Fame. In choosing comics as his medium, he could use Wonder Woman's sagas to show readers the benefits of "becoming more readily accepting of loving submission to loving authorities rather than being so assertive with their destructive egos."

It takes mastering acceptance, the good and the bad, to tap into this super power.

Tarot: The Hanged Man

The Hanged Man is the card of ultimate surrender, of sacrifice for the greater good. He advises us to accept and surrender to our present circumstances because, once when we realise that there are some things we just can't change, that is when we are free from our worries and anxiety. The expression on the man's face shows us that he is tied to the tree of his own will; he has chosen to forsake temptations of instant gratification for a higher cause - he is completely selfless. The card signifies the need to consider the areas of our lives where we could be more selfless - to benefit others or even fulfil our deeper needs. We should always be willing to lose something lesser to accomplish a greater goal.

Illustration:

A dandelion floats freely through the air. A journey through the dark backdrop of forest and forage may provoke fear, but this path represents the need for acceptance of things that are beyond our control. The dandelion accepts the wind, irrespective of the force, as it makes its way back to earth to ultimately reseed. The journey may be varied and difficult, but the end result is the same.

Three quick tips:

- Realise that you cannot control everything. Identify what it is you can control or influence and focus on that
- Look at the situation objectively and without emotion
- Learn to offer forgiveness

A moment of gratitude makes a difference in your attitude.

- Bruce Wilkinson

Chapter Eighteen
Gratitude

Venice

The first time I visited Venice, I still had a full head of wavy blond locks somewhere between a Matthew McConaughey and a James Dean. One might joke that my receding hairline was in part due to the Queen of The Adriatic herself. Either way, somewhere between the wide-eyed excitements of that first trip, to somewhere around the 23rd, there's a parallel to be drawn between the loss of hair and the loss of love or appreciation for Venice, which, over-priced and overcome with throngs of tourists, began to feel like a theme park.

Walking into St Mark's Square for the first time is quite the experience. The surroundings instantly transported me to scenes from the silver screen, like *Moonraker* and *Don't Look Now*.

The fact the city's patron saint is my namesake gave me another reason to celebrate and appreciate the wondrous metropolis where St Mark's symbol, the winged lion, is everywhere. Around 828AD St Mark's remains were stolen from the city of Alexandria by a couple of sneaky little merchants from Venice. Legend has it they replaced the stolen parts with layers of pork.

The current grand Basilica of St Mark is opulent in design and grand in mosaic and decoration. It's also decorated with other famous trophies that were also stolen by the merchants of Venice, such as St Mark's horses that were supposedly originally from the Hippodrome of Constantinople.

Walking around St Mark's Basilica, it's easy to see that Venice is sinking. This, in part, is due to the location of the city's original founding. The Veneti tribe (from where we get the name Venice) moved into areas of the lagoon back in the 5th Century. They built homes on wooden platforms over the wet and swamplands. They believed it was a way of escaping the ravages of war and attacks from the likes of Attila the Hun. It worked, and the city later flourished. However, their location of choice pays the price now, with buildings sinking and water levels rising.

The first time you experience the rising waters, it's quaint. You simply roll up your trouser legs, take off your shoes, then kick, splash and frolic through the uniqueness of it all. After witnessing floods on a couple of occasions, though, my perspective changed. I decided to join the locals who walk on temporary pavements made from wooden planks. The feral waters – sometimes dotted with dead, marinating pigeons – kind of take away from the romanticism of the floods.

Even the famous Venice pigeons lose appeal over time. On my first trip, I was happy to be a seed-covered human perch, attracting the happy flying locals. Apparently being crapped on by a pigeon in Venice is a sign of good luck, but after many trips to the dry cleaner, it feels like the only good luck is if the pigeons leave you alone.

More serious events may have somewhat corrupted my overall opinion towards the city. One of the most difficult times on all the tours I led was having three passengers run over by the same car.

Yes, in a city of bridges, a city famed for canals, three passengers were run over by the same driver.

The high level of theft (of which the first merchants of Venice would be proud), was just one more thing to turn me off the city. Every time I visited Venice with a group of tourists, someone would have something stolen: shopping bags, handbags, backpacks, and even passports.

Glass making, a beautiful art originating on the island of Murano, is wondrous to behold. Skilled artisans blow and shape glass in minutes, turning blobs of molten materials into great forms. The complex, ancient craft of lace making also originates in Venice. The beautiful patterns and designs are a testament to the patience of needlework. The lace works are fascinating and make for great souvenirs. The only problem with the lace and glass is that they are priced for the efforts of the talented craftsmen, yet some passengers found stickers on the packaging saying 'Made in China'. Not so easy to explain.

Around my 23rd trip after doing the city orientation, I began telling people to simply wander and not worry so much about getting lost because clear signs always lead you back to St Mark's Square, our central meeting point for all activities. As the group left, I realised that, while happy, they weren't exuberant the way I had been on my first visit. Then, after speaking with a couple of the passengers I realised that while my impression of Venice was sinking, I had subconsciously transferred my lack of enthusiasm to my passengers. I vowed to be consciously positive in future, even while giving subtle warnings to watch their belongings, so that they could experience the city through naïve and wondrous eyes, and I could benefit too. Because no matter how hot, overcrowded, overpriced or overhyped the city has become, it's still Venice. It's amazing. And how fortunate am I to have the ability to travel and spend time there regularly. After my epiphany, my passion for the place was re-ignited, and I would pro-actively seek out new experiences: venturing over to the beach at Lido, taking long leisurely lunches in rooftop cafés with colleagues and friends, and even knocking back Bellinis at famous Harry's Bar – one of Ernest Hemingway's regular watering holes.

It's amazing how many people, when asked to reflect on their total experience of Europe, allow one slightly sub-standard hotel to interfere with their overall perspective. You'd think substantial exposure to Europe's culture, class, wealth, beauty, museums, sights and cuisines you'd have more to focus on an obscure hotel that was slightly too far out or too small.

Adopt an attitude of gratitude and learn to love the ebb and flow of life. There is plenty of science and research to suggest that doing so can improve physical health, psychological or mental wellness and even our adaptability and strength. Being grateful enhances the quality of relationships. Gratitude invokes concepts like random acts of kindness and thus positively impacts the broader community. To borrow a simple idea from the movie *About Time*, consider living each day with conscious and deliberate gratitude, "as if this were your final day." Let's not forget that less stress might also prevent the recession of hair.

Share more compliments. Be more appreciative. Be more accepting. Say thank you more frequently. You'll be more likely to enjoy the little moments, because whether they are exciting or anxiety inducing, all of them, when forged and fused together with an attitude of gratitude, create a feeling of being on the great roller coaster ride that is your extraordinary life.

Tarot: Wheel of Fortune

The Wheel of Fortune is symbolic of luck, timing, synchronicity, and coincidence. It's a sign to take a chance when unexpected opportunities come knocking. The wheel represents the cycle of life - the continuous cycle of both positive and negative experiences. The card's associating planet is Jupiter, the planet of opportunity, growth, success and expansion. Drawing the card is a reminder that even if you are going through a difficult phase, there will come a time when you will be able to feel at ease and enjoy yourself again. You need to accept that life has ups and downs, and learn to be appreciative of them all. After all, when things seem at their worst, it means they can only get better!

Illustration:

The traditional "Namaste" is a sign of respect and reverent salutation that translates to "bowing to you." The hands graciously clasped in gratitude are decorated with intricate story patterns of henna: capturing the complex web of total experiences. In the background we see a reference to the traditional Tarot in the form of a glorious, stylised sun. The magnificent swirling rays are the turning tides of peaks and troughs, signifying life's ups and downs. The grateful hands show appreciation for them all.

Three quick tips:

- Be thankful for both good and bad experiences – look for the positive in all experiences
- Show appreciation daily
- Start a gratitude journal where you list 10 things per day, no matter how trivial, that you are grateful for

Authenticity requires a certain measure of vulnerability, transparency, and integrity.

- Janet Louise Stepenson

Chapter Nineteen
Authenticity

The three-sided triangle of authenticity

In three short observations, drafted as a mini allegro, I'll explain why we should turn our attention to the triangle players and what we can learn from them.

First Movement: The quiet achievers

Meanwhile, back in at the Mozart performance in Vienna…

The conductor walks in: Enthusiastic applause.

The conductor takes a bow: Very enthusiastic applause.

The conductor presents the Maestro violin: Ecstatic applause (no one has done anything yet).

On completion of each masterpiece: Massive applause (well earned).

Singers are presented: Enthusiastic applause.

Sonatas hammered out: Massive applause.

Singers take a second bow: Ecstatic applause.

Lead violin, singers and conductor all present each other in a humbling round of, "No, really, it's you": Off the Richter, the crowd goes wild.

There is at least one point where, with a general hand sweeping gesture, the conductor presents and invites the remaining pantaloon-wearing ensemble to stand for acknowledgement.

I would always wonder, though, what about recognising the individual efforts of the back row, far corner? On that last track alone, an uplifting overture of *Die Entführung Aus Dem Serail*, one musician, like a man possessed, spent the entire time thrashing their percussion instrument at a heart attack pace. It was the triangle player. If you listen carefully to a recording of the performance, the constant tinkle of the triangle is what gives the song's vivacious tempo an edge.

Often, when you think of a rock star, the image that comes to mind is someone out front, someone in the limelight, someone who doesn't always exhibit the best behaviour. There are other, more subtle, rock stars out there who are just as deserving of our attention.

The triangle player is a perfect example of a rock star who doesn't require, or even desire, the limelight. Some people sit in the back without causing any fuss. It's easy to overlook them, but without them, the overall performance would surely lose some of its impact.

Second movement: Be a one percenter

These days, rock star status isn't reserved for musicians.

Take Nathan Cayless, for example. As former captain of the Parramatta Eels and captain of the New Zealand team that took out the Rugby League World Cup in 2008, Captain Cayless has some great perspectives on leadership, collaboration, teamwork and achieving results.

During several conversations with him, he described a similar concept to the one I had observed on the operatic stage.

He earned much of his success as a professional athlete and has a great way of recognising, tapping into, and ultimately inspiring others. He describes the athletic equivalent of the triangle player as a "one percenter".

"Basically, the one percenters are those [people who] do not get recognised by the average Joe watching the game," he says.

For example, a support player who runs with the teammate who is carrying the footy "so that instead of him getting belted by three or four players, he only gets tackled by a couple at the most," Nathan continues. This gives everyone the chance to play the ball at greater momentum.

"Whether it's the guy who gets his head down and gets stuck in or the support runner, they likely may not receive any credit as they've basically been silent partners."

In footy, it's easy to think the rock star is the one crossing the line for points and glory. If it weren't for the supporting one percenters, those in the limelight might not have made it there at all.

Everyone can be a one percenter by taking a step back to support someone else, especially those who are more accustomed to holding the limelight.

Third Movement: Rock stars

"If you want to be a rock star or just be famous, then run down the street naked, you'll make the news or something. But if you want music to be your livelihood, then play, play, play and play! Eventually, you'll get to where you want to be."

- Eddie Van Halen, Van Halen

"Every guitarist I would cross paths with would tell me that I should have a flashy guitar, whatever the latest fashion model was and I used to say, 'Why? Mine works, doesn't it? It's a piece of wood and six strings, and it works."

- Angus Young, AC/DC

To be a real rock star, whatever you're doing should make a significant positive impact on the wider community.

In a world turned celebrity and selfie mad, it seems the desire for recognition is stronger than the desire to do something meaningful that happens to gain you attention.

Popularity for popularity's sake doesn't make you a rock star any more than wearing a nice suit, designer dress or accessories give you class. It has to be genuine.

Van Halen and Young are right. There are two ways you can become a rock star:

1: Do anything in a flashy manner just for the recognition

2: Do things you believe in, whether you are recognised for your efforts or not

There's an interesting *Forbes* article titled, 'Where have all the rock stars gone?' written by Michele Catalano. The closing summary is pretty succinct and similar: "Most importantly: the musician must put their music first. Your need to make music must be the sole reason you make music. Being real works. Being a rock star doesn't."

Replace the words musician and music with the most appropriate descriptors for your chosen field, and you're good to go.

Real rock stars consistently perform at their best with whatever tools they have at hand, rather than relying on Fugazi-style flashiness to shine.

The Crescendo: The triangle player

The triangle's simplistic design leads people to think that no skill is required to play it when in fact the opposite is true. If you're doubtful, just type 'Dave Grohl triangle player' into a search engine and watch as one of the top percussionists takes the spotlight to wail on the triangle.

People who master the triangle do it for the love of the instrument and the music, rather than the fame. And if Dave Grohl can take a step back mid-concert to show appreciation for this underrated instrument, then we can also take a step back to consider, and become, a necessary (and authentic) background instrument.

The three-sided triangle of authenticity is a good reminder to stay true to your personality, spirit, and character despite external factors like your social status.

Tarot: Fool

At the beginning of his journey, the Fool has unlimited potential. Drawing the Fool card doesn't mean you are foolish; it is a sign of new beginnings and innocence. It represents the desire to accomplish your goals and have new experiences. The Fool lives a carefree existence; he does whatever he wants, free from worry and anxiety, and he doesn't seem to mind what lies ahead. We are encouraged to follow our hearts, no matter how crazy we look; we need to have faith in ourselves and our motivations and stay true to what we believe.

Illustration:

The Venetian-styled carnival mask indicates that turning up as the real you is important for integrity and fulfillment. It can be easy to hide beneath a façade, portraying a version in order to fit in. Be aware that the mask cloaking your genuine self may appeal to others, but it only serves to prevent us from experiencing the best elements of life.

Three quick tips:

- Do things that you believe in, even if others don't share your passion
- Do things that are fulfilling and morally-sound
- It's okay to want to share your achievements, as long as you also have a no-fuss attitude towards them

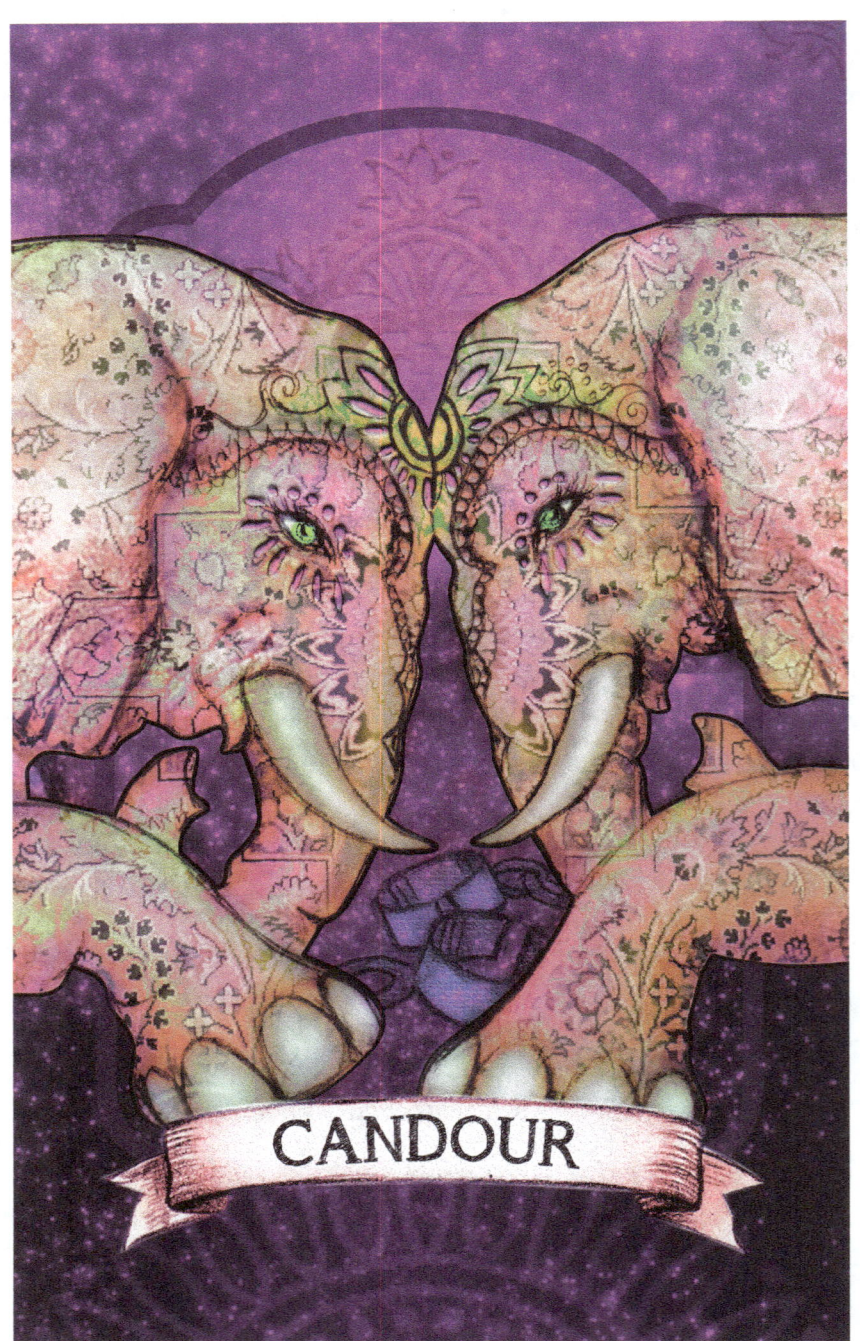

Candour is a compliment; it implies equality. It's how true friends talk.

- Peggy Noonan

Chapter Twenty
Candour

The Elephant in the Room

Ask any zoologist, and they will probably tell you the same thing: elephants don't belong in confined spaces. But there is one species of elephant that does often find itself stuck in a room with no way out. It's the biggest elephant of all, and it's entirely invisible.

In fact, you've probably been in the room while one of these elephants is there. You might not have even noticed it. But when you do realise its presence, you have to be careful not to disturb it. It usually takes more than one person to get an elephant into the room, and once it's in there, these same people tend to ignore it – they don't look at it, they don't speak about it – and that just makes its presence grow.

For the elephant to be set free, those who brought it in need to have an open and honest conversation about why it's there and work together to widen the doorway so it can leave.

This can often be an awkward conversation to have, but by employing candour, you can destroy any mammoth obstacles that are in your way. By speaking candidly, you'll move closer to having a more fulfilling, peaceful and beautiful life. When you speak with candour at every level of your organisation, everything improves – productivity, efficiency, creativity, innovation, and trust.

Live your life with candour

- It's okay to be upset and to say so
- Surround yourself with people who make you feel great and do things that make you smile
- Distance yourself from people or situations that weigh you down
- Staying silent and calm can be more effective than yelling
- Words you scream are lost to the cacophony of noise your actions make
- You may not be able to control others or external situations, but you always have self-control
- Ultimately, it's not what happens that's important; it's how you choose to respond
- Take responsibility for all aspects of your life: words, actions, health, well-being and general happiness
- When you break promises or lie, your word becomes worthless
- Commitment and trust only retain their value when backed by actions
- If you hate your job, either change it or find something to love about it
- Follow your motivation and inspiration
- When it comes to making an important decision, intuition can be just as valid as logic
- Planning something simple can be just as grand a gesture as the most dazzling act of spontaneity
- If someone tells you that you can't do something, it's indicative of their limitations, not yours
- If you have an issue or conflict brewing with someone, tell him or her
- If you like someone, show him or her. Eliminate the games. Say it straight
- If someone tells you that they like you, be flattered

- Realise you don't need to have an opinion on absolutely everything
- Sometimes it's best just to stop talking
- Ask the quietest person in the room for their opinion and listen without interrupting
- Celebrities aren't the only interesting people in the world. There are other people worth listening to (yourself included)
- Muscles alone don't make you strong. Displaying real depth from your core is more important than looking good
- Crying isn't a sign of weakness
- Recognising a broad range of emotions liberates the soul
- Respect the perspectives and traditions of others
- Everyone is born equal and has the right to a peaceful and beautiful life
- Display models, values, and virtues that contribute to a civilised society
- Disagreements should be resolved with words, not weapons
- Being classy is all about your behaviour, rather than designer labels (yes, including Louboutins)
- Speaking of shoes, always walk a mile in someone else's. It will help you to understand why they do the things they do
- The visible demonstration of intelligence is underpinned by observation, empathy, and taking time to pause to think before speaking
- Life is complicated, but a lot of people go out of their way to make it more convoluted
- Hone in on your ability to face the mirror (see Chapter Six), be truthful with yourself, control yourself, challenge yourself, and aspire for goals that are right for yourself and others
- Have empathy for others and a willingness to communicate authentically

The Biggest Dirty Little Secret

When you become comfortable with frankness, you create a space for wins. With regards to candour, Jack Welch is a champion. In fact, he says that a lack of candour is the biggest dirty little secret in business. "What a huge problem it is," he says. "Lack of candor basically blocks smart ideas, fast action, and good people contributing all the stuff they've got. It's a killer."

If you're not familiar with Jack Welch, he was chairman and CEO of General Electric for a period of 20 years between 1981 and 2001. During his tenure of leadership the company's value rose by approximately 4000%. His retirement payout, just a tad shy of half a billion dollars, is one of the largest severance handshakes in history. A straight shooter himself, its easy to see why Jack Welch strived to embed the philosophy of candour and openness in all companies under his umbrella. It's no easy task when you're going against people's long-held behaviours, attitudes and habits.

Honesty can be a little unnerving, and directness can be mistaken for aggressive confrontation. Yet, as Welch says, "When you've got candor — and you'll never completely get it, mind you — everything just operates faster and better."

In Welch's opinion, a lack of candor doesn't necessarily equate to "malevolent dishonesty." It can just mean withholding constructive criticism, or keeping your opinion to yourself to make people feel better and avoid conflict.

Tarot: The High Priestess

The High Priestess sits at the gate before Mystery, with the Tree of Life in the background. She's sitting in the darkness and the light as the mediator of the passage into the depth of reality. Her blue robe represents knowledge, and the cross on her breast is a symbol of the balance between male and female. In her lap is the Torah, representative of the exoteric and esoteric teachings and higher knowledge. The moon under her left foot is symbolic of her dominion over pure intuition, and the palm is indicative of the fertility of the mind. She is the symbol for all that is unknown. When you draw the High Priestess card, you receive an invitation to look within yourself for the truth.

Illustration:

In Hindi religion Ganesha is the patron of wisdom, letters and learning. He captures the concept of mastering the communication skills required in the application of candour. Ganesha's elephant head makes him an easy figure to identify. The nature of this feature also adds an ideal visual storytelling element signifying the importance of calling out the "elephants in the room." At the feet of the majestic mammoths, lies the broken shackles of bureaucracy, conditioning, guardedness, fear of judgment, and false politeness which has previously inhibited or rendered the most important conversations and words unspoken. The elephants face each other respectfully as equals.

Three quick tips:

- If something is bothering you, share it with the right person
- Don't avoid difficult conversations
- Make time for face-to-face conversations

I've learned that people will forget what you said, people will forget what you did, but people will never forget how you made them feel.

- Maya Angelou

Chapter Twenty One
Kindness

Two common languages

We all know humans have changed and evolved since early Homo sapiens wandered the Earth, but exactly what has changed is hard to answer. Many studies suggest our prehistoric ancestors exhibited some of these traits:

- They hunted in packs and gathered in groups
- They huddled for warmth
- They lived with and cared for their elders or sick relatives
- They buried and mourned their dead
- They utilised fire and their natural environment including ferns, furs and stone
- They communicated through a simplistic language

Fast forward to modern day:

- We hang out in groups
- We cuddle on the couch for warmth
- We care for family and friends when they are sick
- We bury or cremate our dead
- Although we rely heavily on technology, we are still able to survive off the environment
- There are many hundreds of complex languages in the world and many people can speak more than one

It's evident that while the essence of our behaviour hasn't changed, the way we communicate has. Where our ancestors spent most of their time interacting within the confines of a small tribe, we are now able to sit behind a computer screen, alone, and communicate with people across the globe.

It's estimated that there are 6,909 languages across Earth's 196 countries. Around 200 of those languages are found in Europe. There is a whopping 2197 vernaculars found in Asia.

And that's not even taking into account all the new languages we've created from these existing languages, like coding and social media speak. But even when we're all speaking the same language, people prefer different aspects of that language, which can make it difficult to communicate. For example, creative types are excited by inspirational words, while the logicians among us prefer words that have depth and many layers of meaning.

So how can we reach and understand one another? You can strip back the layers of communication to reveal two common languages that everyone understands: Kindness and love. These two languages have nothing to do with the words that come out of your mouth. These two languages are universal; they transcend language.

They have more to do with what you do and how you go about doing it; they're associated with your attitude and behaviour. We communicate kindness through service. I'm not speaking of professional service; it has more to do with the services you offer for which you don't get paid. Kindness is a language even the deaf can hear and the blind can see.

As Muhammad Ali said, "Service to others is the rent you pay for your room here on earth."

We all do service to others every day. Learn to recognise which services you perform, and which you enjoy. Being able to see the joy in service can be a fulfilling experience.

Use Napoleon Hill's QQS formula as your guide:

Quality: Is your service conducted in an efficient manner with others in mind?

Quantity: Are you capable of performing more services?

Spirit: Do you have a friendly attitude and are you willing to work in harmony with others? This can often make up for deficiencies in other areas.

Tarot: World

The World card shows a dancing figure and rejoicing in the completion of her journey and the new beginnings that lay ahead. She is the opposite of the Hanged Man because where he looks inward, she looks outward. The red ribbons on her wreath symbolise the immense rewards of improving ourselves and, as a result, those around us. Like The Wheel of Fortune, the World card reflects the cyclical progression of time and human experience. To draw this card means all your efforts are paying off, and the hardships you have endured along the way have been worth it because you are smarter, wiser and more experienced than you were when you started out. It shows that everything has come together and is how it should be. It also shows a strong desire to give something back to the larger community.

Illustration:

The world is being nurtured by a set of hands that belong to everyone. The world is a celebration of self, harmony with others, and a greater awareness of our choices and their ripple effect.

Three quick tips:

- Reflect upon past mistakes and make amends
- Do something for someone each day without the need for recognition
- Offer some time, help, effort or energy to a philanthropic cause, a social project or something within the community

Dream without fear. Love without limits.

- Unknown

Chapter Twenty Two
Love

Sorrento: European training tour

March 2001

I was drawing a simple map on Paolo's slightly used napkin. Corso Italia, Via Degli Aranci and Via Correale. These three parallel lines then curved to meet each other. The napkin was to become coach directions for our Sorrento tour (Google Maps wouldn't be launched for another four years, so hand written notes were how we stayed on track).

Senior Paolo Fortini had been drawing these streets for years, and I mimicked his method, right down to theatrically tapping the pen on the section of road that read 'No Entry' and impersonating his deep voice while saying, "Whatever you do. Do not. Go down. That road!"

That's no grammatical error. Paolo frequently delivered messages with importance and pause. It ensured his audience's attention. In fact, if you were to picture Jean Reno as the Italian diver, Enzo Molinari, in *The Big Blue* and add a healthy moustache and huge eyebrows, you would be pretty close to Senior Fortini.

Paolo then let out a booming laugh and grabbed my shoulder in the same manner with which he seemed to handle many aspects of life:

with a very firm grip. He embraced me across the table, as one might a naughty nephew, and tears of laughter formed in his eyes. He sat back casually in his seat, tapping his chest as his laughter changed to a steady chortle. He wiped his eyes, then once again took the conversational reigns.

Paolo was always a wonderful storyteller. I'd known him for many years by this stage, so I knew the tale he was preparing to tell me would be different this time. This was the moment Senior Paolo enlightened me with what he believed constituted a fulfilling life.

He delivered his words of wisdom in a deep, booming Italian accent. "Mark," he said. His digression from the informal Marco he usually called me immediately caught me off guard. He paused. My ears pricked up. I was now an eager, cross-legged listener who was about to hear his master's secret. Once he knew my attention was absolute, he continued.

"Mark. There are three things. Every man. Must do. In a lifetime." He slowly raised three fingers on his right hand and straightened the lapel of his jacket with his left. The whole movement was dramatised by a lift of his bushy eyebrows to reveal wide, intense eyes.

"One: Plant a tree." He nodded and lowered one finger quickly as if this was something I should already know.

"Two: Write a book." He raised his eyebrows as if to make sure I fully understood, then added," Every man. Has in him. A book."

"And what should this book be about, Paolo?"

He gave a flippant wave of his left hand and said, "The subject is irrelevant. Just write the book, Mark." He lowered his second finger and his eyebrows returned to their regular place.

"Three." This pause was unusually long, even by Paolo's standards. He reeled in his third finger and leaned in, lowering his voice but giving a wry smile. "Raise a child."

To me, that third instruction was an obvious way to live a fulfilled life. I realised he had given me the instructions in the order they give out Olympic medals – gold last. He did this because, to Paolo, the most important thing in life was family.

The first time I told this story was after I learnt of his passing in 2010. The last time I had seen him was in 2007, and the time before that was 2001. I had been living in Florence for a year when I met Paolo and his band of merry locals back in 1995. They added an element of warmth to a the city I already loved, making my time there one of the most rewarding experiences of my life.

I've had very few mentors in my life – I could count them on one hand – and Senior Fortini was one of them. Fortinisms and philosophies sneak their way into my training programs and keynote speeches. One of my favourites is his jaded opinion on leadership. He always said that people should take the word "super" out of their titles and simply call themselves "visor" because, in his words, "There's nothing f**king super about them!"

Love or fear

It may seem like there are hundreds of thousands of emotions (you're probably feeling a few right now), but in essence, they are all just variations on love or fear.

Elisabeth Kübler-Ross, a Swiss-American psychiatrist said it best:

> *There are only two emotions: love and fear. All positive emotions come from love, all negative emotions from fear.*

From love flows happiness, contentment, peace, and joy. From fear comes anger, hate, anxiety and guilt. It's true that there are only two primary emotions, love and fear. But it's more accurate to say that there is only love or fear, for we cannot feel these two emotions together, at exactly the same time. They're opposites. If we're in fear, we are not in a place of love. When we're in a place of love, we cannot be in a place of fear.

Love and fear are at opposite ends of the spectrum. If you're ever unsure about which end you're closer to, simply take the time to check in with your emotions, and remember:

- Fear is blame based. Love is accepting
- Fear drives a desire to control. Love allows freedom and detachment
- Fear kills passion or a desire to succeed. Love enlivens and ignites it
- Fear is the saboteur trying to prevent you from making positive changes
- Love is the super hero that makes everything possible
- Love is the energy that expands. Fear is the energy that contracts
- Every single event is an opportunity to learn to choose love over that fear

The holistic concept of love

The reason I opened this chapter with the Sorrento story was because the wisdom from the short anecdote shows us not only how to live a fulfilling life, but one that is based on love.

I agree with Paolo, everyone has a book in them especially if they are following a path they love. Planting a tree shows love for the environment and your community. And raising a child with your partner is the ultimate show of love: a love only a parent can know.

Below are some Fortinisms we can apply to every day life:

1: Love is for expression not impression

The most important 'like' you receive every day should be the smile you give yourself as you catch your reflection in the mirror. This is a sign of loving and respecting yourself in a healthy way: it's not conceit or narcissism.

- Be humble in your confidence and courageous in your character.
- Confidence, self-control, and attitude are among the most attractive qualities an individual can have.
- Focus on wellness by looking after mind, body and spirit. How could you expect anyone else to see your beauty if you can't elevate yourself? This becomes an easier path to follow when you truly love and value yourself.
- Being present, and letting go of any toxins which you may have been clinging to. Replace the toxins with uplifting tonics.
- Honest self-reflection translates into powerful and effective decision-making. The tough choices in life become easier when you reach a heightened level of awareness that needs no approval or validation from outside the walls of the self. The ego can, well, go.

2: Love is for a cause, not applause

Being adaptable as situations and opportunities arise can lead you down a rewarding life path. Line your path with goals that intrinsically motivate and inspire you. Remain productive, consistent and creative in pursuit of them.

There's a segment in the documentary *Happy* where Dr Tim Kasser says that there are two intrinsic motivators when it comes to happiness:

Extrinsic motivators – outside of oneself:

- Financial success
- Image
- Status and popularity

Intrinsic motivators – satisfying in and of themselves:

- Personal growth
- Relationships
- Desire to make the world a better place

Studies show those who are driven by intrinsic motivators show more vitality, fulfillment and overall happiness in comparison to those who derive motivation from external factors. Success and wealth can certainly add both comfort and fulfillment in life, yet the message is clear: don't be too focussed on materiality.

Choose a path that suits your natural talents and one that also leaves a positive impact on the world. The greatest level of personal fulfillment invariably comes through collaboration with others. When you have a definitive purpose, you're more motivated to step up to any challenges that arise.

3: Love yourself

Forget trying to find the one thing or that one person you believe will make you happy. Instead, remain focussed on being the best version of yourself. You're a self-polishing diamond, with infinite inner strength.

4: Romantic love

Lastly, there's butterflies-in-the-stomach, head-spinning, romantic love. Which is possibly the scariest thing of all. Here are some things to remember:

- "Love is the total absence of fear. Love asks no questions. Its natural state is one of extension and expansion, not comparison and measurement." – Gerald Jampolsky
- "Love takes off masks that we fear we cannot live without and know we cannot live within." – James Baldwin
- "Don't let the sadness of your past or the fear of your future ruin the happiness of your present." - Unknown
- "If you want to know love you must allow the armour of fear to be stripped from you, piece by piece, until you are naked before the world." – Teal Scott

When you learn to accept that some things are out of your control, you can begin to live in the present moment. Live life with gratitude and authenticity, and the right person will ultimately find, see and choose you.

Relationships, including deep lasting friendships, can be established fairly quickly, yet building trust to the point where you can speak to each other with candour is what will help your relationship stand the test of time. Treat others with care, respect and kindness, and always operate from a place of love.

Love or fear? That is the decision that defines you.

Tarot: The Lovers

The Lovers are blessed and protected by the angel Raphael, the angel of air. Air represents communication, an essential element for a healthy relationship. The sun brings warmth and security, and the earth suggests fertility and happiness. There is a snake in a tree in the background, which is a nod to the story of Adam and Eve and all earthly temptations. The man looks at the woman while the woman looks at the angel, signifying the path from physical desire to emotional needs to spiritual concerns. The mountain is a phallic symbol, and the flames come from a fire of passion. The Lovers represent trust between two people, and the ability to help one another overcome life's obstacles.

Illustration:

The illustration captures the holistic definition of love: love yourself, love others, love what you do, love your community and environment in addition to the romantic sense of the word. Lovers bonding together become entwined with and a part of the intricate tree of life.

Three quick tips:

- Above all else, find a way to love and value yourself
- Do what you love and love what you do
- Give 100% to every relationship, including friendship

Prologue

Classic perspectives related to character

In 1937 Napoleon Hill completed a body of work he'd been working on for close to a decade. Inspired by input from business magnate and philanthropist Andrew Carnegie, he'd been on a research journey to identify key ingredients to success.

A section of the book highlights the common characteristics of successful leaders in fields such as business, science, sport, politics, philanthropy, and entertainment

You can use the checklist to form a solid basis for self-reflection and self-improvement.

- Unwavering courage
- Self-control
- Keen sense of justice
- Definiteness of decision
- A pleasing personality
- Sympathy and understanding
- Mastery of detail
- A willingness to assume full responsibility and accountability
- Cooperation

Angels and demons: qualities and the culmination of character

As a movie lover, it seemed appropriate to take advice from some of the silver screen's greatest characters.

Villains and the traits to avoid:

10: The Evil Queen from *Snow White and the Seven Dwarfs*
You'll never be the apple of anyone's eye if you display vanity and envy.

9: Regan MacNeil from *The Exorcist*
Aggression will cause people to think you're behaving like the Devil.

8: Phyllis Dietrichson from *Double Indemnity*
Being manipulative is nothing short of murderous.

7: Alex Forrest from *Fatal Attraction*
Obsession, with a touch of an addictive nature, means temperatures, friendships (and possibly cute bunnies) will ultimately be boiled.

6: Henry F. Potter from *It's a Wonderful Life*
The moral of the story: if you're selfish and a scrooge, in the end, you'll lose.

5: Nurse Ratched from *One Flew Over the Cuckoos Nest*
Don't be power hungry and cold.

4: The Wicked Witch of The West from *The Wizard of Oz*
There's no magic to being rotten.

3: Darth Vader from *Star Wars*
   Anger and ego are temptations from the dark side.

2: Norman Bates from *Psycho*
   Be careful of the traits you are teaching your children.

1: Dr. Hannibal Lecter from *Silence of the Lambs*
   Being a sociopath will only eat you up.

Heroes and the traits to replicate:

10: British Lieutenant T.E. Lawrence from *Lawrence of Arabia*
    Be modest and loyal.

9: George Bailey from *It's A Wonderful Life*
   A selfless, kind nature and a keen sense of social justice means George's guardian angel was protecting him, right there by his side.

8: Ellen Ripley from *Alien*
   Being determined and decisive made her the saviour of human kind.

7: Rocky Balboa from *Rocky*
   "It ain't how hard you get hit, it's about how hard we can get hit and keep moving forward."

6: Clarice Starling from *Silence of The Lambs*
   Being brave, sympathetic and endearingly human can soften even the hardest heart.

5: Will Kane from *High Noon*
   A sense of duty and honour is important in the face of adversity.

4: Rick Blaine from *Casablanca*
   Sometimes you need to make sacrifices.

3: James Bond from *James Bond 007*
   Stay cool, calm and collected.

2: Indiana Jones from *Raiders of The Lost Ark*
   Being intellectual and humble can whip you into shape.

1: Atticus Finch from *To Kill a Mockingbird*
   Honesty, combined with a high sense of morality, a lack of prejudice, authenticity, and a keen sense of justice are virtues.

   - 'Character, not circumstances, makes the person.' - Booker T Washington.
   - 'Character is how you treat those who can do nothing for you.' – Unknown
   - 'The truth of your character is exposed through the choice of your actions.' – Dr Steve Maraboli

Illustration:

Who we show up as influences the perception of others. We clearly favour characters who bring the light, and who are more saintly and angelic, rather than a devil in disguise.

Passion is born when you catch a glimpse of your potential.

– Zig Ziglar

Questions to ask yourself in order to find your passion:

- What inspires me?
- What makes me happy?
- What makes me lose track of time?
- To where does my mind drift when I daydream?
- What would I do if money and energy were endless?

Passion:

The second of the two illustrations, this female *Vitruvian Man* once again features 22 sun rays, but here they represent the inner soul. This card symbolises the practical, grounded, pragmatic application of the tools mentioned in this book.

About the Author

Twenty years ago Mark Carter (MC) worked as a tour director, industry trainer and leader across Europe for Contiki Holidays and Travcorp. Today he is a sought-after international presenter and trainer based in Australia.

Mark approaches the subjects of peak performance, transformational leadership and personal development with a unique perspective and depth that comes from leading thousands of people, hundreds of thousands of kilometres across a continent. He's additionally held senior strategic development roles, consulting for billion dollar businesses and small- to medium-sized enterprises covering industries such as e-commerce, travel, recruitment, advertising, telecommunications, banking, insurance, hospitality, health, government and not-for-profit.

Mark has serendipitously acquired a catalogue of experiences many people dream about. This innovative knowledge is further cemented through professional certifications and accreditations. His anecdotes and style serve to take participants on a journey; dismantling complex concepts into appropriately bite sized, pragmatic strategies and tools.

Born in England, fermented in Scotland, nurtured by Europe and matured through several round-the-world trips, he now calls Australia home and enjoys the fruits of a sunny lifestyle. Mangoes, after all, don't grow in Edinburgh.

Comments Regarding MC's Style

'What Mark does to captivate his audience is he makes them think. Rather than just giving them the answers, he asks the questions and takes them on a journey with him.'

'Mark Carter should be bottled and drunk daily!'

'Inspirational. Keeps it real. Energetic!'

IGNITING YOUR POTENTIAL

The book ties into our first public development program. Igniting Your Potential is a body of work designed with essential ingredients derived from successful programs that have been delivered in corporate environments for close to two decades. The program is underpinned by behavioural science modelling as part of a rich collection of pragmatic tools to tap peak performance and masterful communication. The program is divided into four chapters: Ignite Your Potential, Ignite To Evolve, Ignite Your Flow, and Ignite To Flourish.

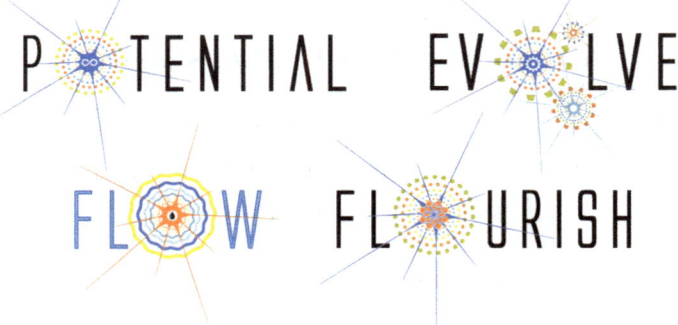

Join the newsletter and social media for development insights. Get a bespoke handmade dreaMCatcher through periodic giveaways. Illustrations can be purchased on the website.

markcarter.com.au
Instagram - @ignitingyourpotential
Facebook - Mark Carter - Igniting Human Potential

www.ingramcontent.com/pod-product-compliance
Lightning Source LLC
Chambersburg PA
CBHW050536300426
44113CB00012B/2131